Scarlet Song

Mariama Bâ

Translated by Dorothy S Blair
with a glossary and notes

 LONGMAN

Pearson Education Limited,
Edinburgh Gate, Harlow
Essex CM20 2JE, England
and Associated Companies throughout the world

Longman Publishers USA
10 Bank Street
White Plains
New York 10601-1951
USA

Copp Clark Pitman Ltd
2775 Matheson Blvd East
Mississauga
Ontario L4W 4P7
Canada

First published 1981 by Les Nouvelles Editions Africanes
First Published in Longman African Classic 1986
First Published in Longman African Writers 1994
Twenty-third impression 2008

Set in Baskerville

Printed in Malaysia, PJB

ISBN 978-0-582-26455-7

In memoriam

'They stand poised on the springboard and leap into the void; God gathers them in his hand, bears them through the air, softens their fall.' These words by the poet Jean Sarment come inevitably to mind when we think of Mariama Bâ who disappeared 'in full flight'. At the Frankfurt Book Fair in October 1980, she became the centre of attraction for one week as the representative and spokeswoman for all African literature, when the first Noma Prize for publishing in Africa was awarded for her novel, *Une si longue lettre (So long a letter)*. Immediately after her return home, she experienced the first symptoms of the malignant disease that was to carry her off less than a year later, in August 1981.

Mariama Bâ's first work remains the brightest jewel in the crown of our publishing house; but in deploring the loss of one of our authors, we mourn even more the loss of a sunny-natured friend, a generous-hearted individual, who had adopted as her personal cause the defence of women in our developing societies.

The reader will find in *Scarlet Song* a crusade against social injustices; but the author also pleads the case for pride in individual identities, although the negative aspects of these do not escape her.

Mariama Bâ was aware that she was dying. This great-hearted woman never rebelled or cursed her fate during her short calvary. She wept sometimes, but her Islamic faith had taught her to accept an unjust fate. So we must be resigned, as she was, to her early passing, but nothing can still our regrets.

Les Nouvelles Editions Africaines

To my uncle, Ousmane Macoumba Diop

In the Harmattan's turbulence,
The intensity of prayers!
In the winding paths of memory,
Messages faintly gleam!

Our forebears, Ma Ngoye and Mademba Ngoye,
Amid the warriors' wild stamping feet
Heard each one his tom-tom's thundrous beat,
Symbol of valour and of eminence.

Coumba Dior Diaw,
Lion woman,
Sleep in the solemn peace of Soumbedioune,
Ringed with radiance, Diop Mao.

From this long line, extolled by the griots of Ndande
Will spring a new young shoot
Worthy custodian
Of ancestral virtue and piety.

As I lend my ear to the voices of our dead
The fevers of the past pervade my thoughts!
My fond heart was strengthened by your affection:
You filled the void of my orphaned childhood.

Mariama Bâ

PART ONE

1

The district of Grand Dakar known as Usine Niari Talli takes its name from the two parallel main roads that run through it and the Biscuit Factory in the neighbourhood. Usine Niari Talli was shaking off its nocturnal torpor in the first quiver of morning sunshine, and objects resumed their normal shapes and colours as the last shadows faded.

Ousmane was already awake at this hour. He lay abed in a delightful state of drowsiness, his eyes half-open, conscious of all the sounds around him which he tried to identify in his mind...

Flip flop! Flip flop! That would be Yaye Khady's footsteps! Flip flop! Flip flop! Her footsteps made their purposeful way towards his window...

A tap, another tap, several taps, each followed by the urgent repetition of the diminutive of his name: 'Oussou!'

'Oussou! Oussou!' The staccato drumming persisted, drawing from him intermittent mutters that became gradually more articulate, helping him to overcome the last vestiges of his inertia.

And so he finally emerged from his rumpled blankets, yawned, stretched, yawned again, collected his sandals and unbolted his door.

Then he made his way to the shower-hut in the corner of the yard, enclosed by rusty sheets of galvanised iron and paved with black stones.

His mother had left warm water for him to help him in his morning toilet, for the icy wind, flapping against the sheets of galvanised iron, paralysed his fingers. As he rubbed himself dry he felt his heart beating a little faster: a new academic year was beginning.

To start the new term he chose an African caftan of embroidered Lagos cotton, which had brought him good luck in the final school exams, and changed from his sandals into closed shoes.

As usual, at this hour, his father had already left the house: his voice could be heard in prayer, mingled with the chorus of the faithful at the mosque.

Yaye Khady was sharing out the bread for breakfast in the court-yard. She glanced furtively at her eldest son's bush of hair. 'Aren't you having any breakfast? The kinkeliba's hot.'

3

Ousmane shook his head. 'You know I never eat anything in the morning when I've got classes, Ma.'

Yaye Khady shrugged her shoulders. 'You're starting a new school! You can just as well start a new habit!'

A brief exchange between a son in a hurry to be off and a mother concerned for his welfare, and Ousmane was already in the street.

The street! Its rhythms and colours! Already people were swarming along the two thoroughfares that ran through the district.

To save on fares, an important item in his family, Ousmane had decided never to travel by bus.

He calculated the length of his new journey. 'So, I shall control my pace, walking slower or faster according to the time at my disposal.'

This year he had a longer distance to travel. 'So what! I'll just have to get up earlier, when I hear the rattle of Pa's kettle for his ablutions, instead of waiting for my brother's sniffling or the flip-flop of Ma's sandals.'

He was used to walking. Over the ten years that he had been walking to school, he had learned the secret of overcoming the distance. He forgot the miles as he 'flirted' with the street.

The street! It was life and light, as familiar to Ousmane as an old and trusted friend. He was sensitive to its needs and could list its characteristics. He could assign to each locality its specific troubles and was always in tune with its moods which varied with the season or the time of day.

The street was the city's essential connecting link, tolerating, with equal indifference, the proximity of slums and imposing mansions...

What was hidden behind these dilapidated walls at each bend of the road? What stories did these faded old facades have to tell? The humble dwelling and the proud abode alike could shelter domestic harmony or be governed by discord and enmity.

The intimacy of closed shutters...thatched roofs...pink tiles... cracked stones...flower-covered fences...wrought-iron gates... rickety shanties...mud walls...red brick facades...foliage through which breezes murmur! Ousmane walked on and on.

Every morning the madman stood under the same lamp-post, stretching out his hand for alms. The unnatural brightness of his eyes and his tormented gaze were disturbing to the onlooker. Ousmane fled from the spectre, turning his own eyes upward to

4

admire the heavens.

The heavens — that immense expanse where swollen gold and purple clouds drifted interminably. What was the destination and the destiny of those long skeins of birds, which took over each morning from those of the previous day? Would they die in captivity, or perish as victims of the elements?

Ousmane walked on and on. The street had its shocking sights: ragged children huddled in groups or standing all alone, shivering in the November cold; their tear-filled eyes and face ravaged with hunger tugged at the heart-strings of the passers-by. Blind beggars gave utterance to their darkness in moving lamentations. The one-armed, the hunch-backed, the one-legged, all those with any sort of handicap fell back on the generosity of the street: the display of an infirmity awakens pity, pity sparks off the charitable reflex which alleviates misery. Ousmane never slackened his pace. And the street unwound before him, its surface now even, now full of pot-holes. Imposing or vulgar, smart or dusty, busy or quiet, it stretched out, now straight, now winding, sometimes narrower, sometimes widening.

As he walked, Ousmane's mind went back to the past...to his childhood and early schooldays...to the succession of schoolmasters to whose teaching he owed the fact that he was now starting university!

They had instilled in him a love of hard work. They had shown him how the key to success is forged by patience and perseverance.

Djibril Gueye, his father, had contributed to his success, inspiring him with a taste for work, teaching him humility, while firing him with ambition.

'Work is the only path to self-advancement!' he was never tired of repeating, drawing his philosophy from his own hard childhood, spent in the Koranic school, under the pitiless rod of a marabout.

'Our master's daily disquisitions on the divine laws did not quench his thirst for worldly goods!' Djibril Gueye revealed his disillusion. 'According to his system of education, religious instruction was not a priority. His *talibés* were trained primarily for begging.'

When the Second World War broke out, Djibril Gueye was still at this same Koranic school, now relieving the master in instructing the younger boys, as his father had insisted that he stay at the school for the rest of his life, even when he had completed his studies.

In those days a father's word carried more weight than nowadays in dictating a child's fate. Even as adults, offspring would give way to family pressures which were sometimes contrary to their own interests.

The war, bringing a massive recruitment into the Senegalese Rifles from the different territories of the then French West African Colonies, had delivered Djibril Gueye from the marabout's yoke. The war thus freed him from his father's solemn promise, and also broadened his horizons beyond the evening readings from the Koran by the light of a wood fire. Djibril Gueye discovered that other voices filled the earth which were not in opposition to the worship of the Lord.

He had returned from the war with one leg shorter than the other and with numerous decorations. As an ex-serviceman he enjoyed certain privileges in his dealings with the colonial administration; thus, in recognition of his disability and in 'appreciation' of his services, he was granted a small plot of land in Grand-Dakar.

As he had no training for any trade or profession, he spent the greater part of his time in recounting 'his' war, and in denouncing the Germans, 'those *Toubabs* who hated the Blacks and so took it out on the French'.

To his neighbours, he was known as 'The Man who had seen Paris'. This 'good fortune' brought him many friends.

Through the admiration and generous offices of a fellow Muslim, he had been able to obtain a beautiful young wife, Yaye Khady Diop.

Ousmane walked on and on and the distance diminished. He raked through the memories that came bubbling up this morning, from the recesses of his conscious memory, to try to find the reasons for the great admiration that he had always had as a child for his father. Was it his kindliness? His philanthropy? His deep devotion to Islam? Perhaps it had been something far more trivial; maybe his child's eyes had been dazzled by the array of medals that Yaye Khady proudly pinned on the starched white boubou which his father donned once a quarter to go and collect his ex-serviceman's pension.

As Ousmane grew up and compared his father's behaviour with that of others, his admiration for him grew. He accepted Djibril Gueye's philosophy: 'As children reach maturity, they can distinguish honesty from crookery; they learn that an avalanche of reproaches covers the parents' concern for the child's welfare; that behind the parents' severe gaze is hidden their love and their need to protect. As they reach maturity children judge their parents. And their verdict is seldom open to appeal . . .'

Above all, Ousmane was grateful to his father for having resisted the temptation to take more wives. Djibril Gueye was very conscious of his small means, limited to his quarterly pension. But, like many others, he might easily have indulged in three more wives and strained the resources of the smallholding.

His attitude saved him from the nagging anxieties which plagued his neighbour, Pathé Ngom, after they had listened to the Imam's Friday evening sermon: 'A man must be like an evenly balanced scale. He must weigh out in equal measures his compliments and his reproaches. He must give equally of himself. He must study his gestures and behaviour and apportion everything fairly!'

'Those principles are very difficult to put into practice,' commented Ousseynou, Pathé Ngom's eldest son, and Ousmane's 'hut-brother'.

From what Ousseynou confided in him, Ousmane got a very precise idea of what life was like in a polygamous family. 'Every wife has charge of the ''budget'' for the whole compound, every second day. That wife is overwhelmed by the task of making this sum stretch to several meals. Often she has to cadge and scrounge for the wherewithal to flatter the Master of the House's gastronomic tastes. Then, to safeguard her reputation, she sees to it that the best of his leavings go into the dish reserved for the other adults. The children get the worst of this share-out of the contents of the cooking-pot, and as their fingers pick through the coscous or the rice, they find nothing but bones.'

When Ousseynou was invited to the Gueyes' house, he was astonished to find that they ate slowly. At his home none of the children chewed their food; they all gulped it down, trying to snatch as much as possible in the shortest time and so keep up with the grown-ups who, with their 'giant handfuls', always had the lion's share. No-one protested lest he be called a meanie who begrudged sharing his food.

Ousmane had witnessed scenes in Pathé Ngom's compound, caused by the rivalry among his wives. Children sided with their mothers and were dragged into their quarrels, sharing their deep-seated resentment. In these confrontations everything to hand was

7

used as a weapon: the basin full of dirty water, the brazier full of burning coals, the saucepan of boiling water, ladle, pestle, broken bottles.

Ousmane smiled. 'Thank goodness, Yaye Khady is the only "lady" in our compound! She's the only one in charge in her own yard. There, she's the mistress of all she surveys; hers are the only hands that scrub and scour; she can organise everything and if anything goes wrong, she is the one to put it right. Every morning presents her with the day's succession of complex duties, and when these are completed by the evening she has to tackle the same succession again, early the next morning, and so on, day after day.'

As long as Yaye Khady was young and strong, she never complained about the bowls of water she had to carry from the public tap, nor about her eyes reddened by smoke from the fire; nor about the broom that was too short and made her so tired.

'Yaye Khady's heart is like a pitcher of fresh water from which, for as long as I can remember, only father and I have drunk.'

Ousmane smiled again. 'To be sure, life is not always easy. But understanding and affection reign in our hut.'

Thanks to the spacing of her pregnancies — one every five years, 'like an elephant', they murmured in the neighbourhood — Yaye Khady was still in her prime, unlike those women who were worn out by constant child-bearing.

She had no cause to envy her friends whose first-born had been girls. From an early age Ousmane had been prepared to be 'her arms and legs', helping her by fetching the coal and water. What is more, he knew what seasoning to put in the food and he would sneak away from his playmate Ousseynou, so as not to be seen when he undertook the tiring job of sweeping out the house for his mother.

Their frequent intimate conversations had woven an understanding between mother and son that made them both happy.

2

Djibril Gueye was not too happy to see his son constantly at Yaye Khady's side. He never missed an opportunity of lecturing his wife when he came upon Ousmane fanning the fire or sweeping up the rubbish.

'You'll turn the lad into a sissy!' he thundered. And Djibril Gueye pondered more and more on the means of 'rescuing' the youngster from his mother. Remembering the martyrdom he had suffered at the Koranic school he was not encouraged to resort to that solution. He had too vivid a memory of the *talibés* being held down by four stout fellows, while the long whip rained down on their naked backs.

He was tempted by the whitefolk's school. And the father's ambition to assure for his son the best possible character-training turned out to be Ousmane's opportunity.

Year after year he advanced further through the dense forest of knowledge in the French school. Every morning, after first helping his mother with the housework, while his father was still chanting his prayers at the mosque, Ousmane tied his books and writing equipment in an old scarf and raced off so as not to be late for school.

The night-time was his own. He soaked up his first lessons by the light of a storm-lantern placed on the ground. When his bit of chalk was used up, he took a piece of burnt wood to compose new sentences on the wooden floor of his hut, using the new words he had just learnt. Addition and subtraction, multiplication and division, practised and tested every day, held no more secrets for him.

At night, his thirst for knowledge, allied with his love of reading, kept him from his bed. He found older pupils to assist him in his reading. Through his untiring efforts, helped by his exceptional intelligence, he always had good marks to bring home to his parents.

Ousmane recalled the year he took the exam to enter high school. 'Oh! The hours I spent, gazing at Ouleymatou Ngom, with her beauty and charm!'

When their eyes met, he felt a great joy. His heart beat faster, his breathing quickened. He eagerly offered to help her solve a maths problem or apply a rule of French grammar. Sometimes, in the course of these encounters, their fingers would touch, as they

9

bent over their books. But Ouleymatou would quickly withdraw her hand — too quickly for Ousmane's liking — and she would purse up her lips reprovingly.

When they played the game of 'Hunt the stick' in the dark, she saw to it that she searched for the hidden object in the same places as Seydou Niang, Ousseynou's other hut-brother.

This new attitude puzzled Ousmane. Ousseynou, pressed for an explanation, finally admitted, 'My sister doesn't want a boy who sweeps the house, fetches buckets of water and smells of dried fish.'

Ousmane was deeply hurt by these words, and the tears that are so near the surface in an adolescent filled his eyes.

He was tortured with pangs of jealousy. But he had a high concept of dignity, inspired by his father who had always extolled the honour of their ancestors. He was a Gueye, of pure Lebu stock, those who had forged the fame of the Cape Verde peninsular, those who had conquered the ocean to make their fortunes, those who were the familiars of invisible creatures who wielded powers of good and evil — the *rab* and the *tour*.

Whenever his father's friend, the praise-singer Lamine Mboye, recited the long lineage of the Gueye family, he never failed to make the most of that ancestor who had been enterprising enough to seduce a *rab*. When this Gueye woke up the morning after his wedding night, he found his courtyard filled with calabashes of steaming millet-porridge and curdled milk, his invisible bride's contribution to the wedding feast.

What was Ouleymatou, compared with these spirit-brides, who were said to be as beautiful as the moonlight, with huge luminous eyes and long silky hair that hung right down their backs as far as their knees?

Ousmane knew all about the hardships his father had endured at the Koranic school. Djibril Gueye had told him of his misadventures one night when there had been a dense dust storm. He had lost his way coming back from a village where he had lingered to get some fresh rags to cover himself and to beg for a little food. The wind raged about his ears as he struggled desperately through the darkness, his feet sinking into the soft sand. His tattered boubou blew around his thin body, exposing his limbs to the cold air. He laboured on in the gloom, bumping against what he took to be rocks.

Suddenly a blinding flash of lightning lit up his surroundings; with a shudder Djibril discovered that he was wandering about in the village cemetery, among the gravestones. He squatted down, shut his eyes and stayed there till daybreak, calling on his knowledge of the Koran for protection.

When he arrived back, up to his ankles in mud, his ragged clothes drenched through, his temples throbbing with fever, his lamentable state did not spare him from the lashes that now rained in their turn on his back . . .

So should he, Ousmane, weep because a little miss ignored him and preferred the dunce of the class?

Ousmane succeeded in keeping his feelings under control and repressed the budding romantic attachment by dint of pride and will-power.

Ousmane's memories continued as he walked on. He shook his head as he recalled those early emotions, gone with the wind, like his childhood to which they belonged.

Neither Ouleymatou or Ousseynou had passed the rigorous entry examination to high school, whereas Ousmane had passed with a scholarship which had eased the family budget. A tiny den for him was built on to their two-roomed hut. As the years went by, running water was installed which made Yaye Khady's existence easier. Finally electricity came.

Seven years of high school had not lessened Ousmane's enthusiasm for hard work. It was with the same brisk step and the same thirst for knowledge that he made his way to university this morning.

Whenever he had felt himself beginning to fancy any girl, after the Ouleymatou experience, the memory of her mocking indifference and his own disillusionment had made him fiercely determined to nip any emotional attachment in the bud. For him, all women were as selfish, disdainful, pretentious and hard as Ouleymatou. He drew back from any temptation. He imagined all the gossip about him and the sly sniggers this would inspire. He kept his distance to prevent any hurtful whispers of 'That's the young man who used to do the sweeping and go to buy dried fish!'

Even when he was attracted by a girl, he took refuge behind an armour of coolness which protected him from her meaningful glances. His attitude was not an escape. He was on his guard. He would talk politely to girls in his class and sometimes he would help them with their work, but he never showed any particular interest. He never looked a girl in the eye when he talked to her, for fear of being ensnared by that little seductive glimmer which would demolish his good resolutions.

Wary and idealistic, Ousmane feared the feminine wiles which diverted the youth of the neighbourhood. The adventures and mis-adventures of his school-friends encouraged him in his uncompromising attitude. He was simply not interested in women, whom he categorised as flighty and irresponsible, ready to lie and deceive.

Thinking that he had no time for anything but his books, his classmates had nicknamed him 'The Priest'! They had no inkling of the rebuff his first calf-love had brought him and the torment he had endured.

Ousseynou, who shared his secret, like a perfect friend never breathed a word about that episode.

3

Could Ousmane Gueye call his light-hearted encounters with Auntie Kiné's niece a sentimental attachment? Auntie Kiné was a neighbour who was on very good terms with Yaye Khady. On his way home from school he used to pass the niece near the charcoal merchant's, carrying her blackened basket on her arm.

This child haunted Yaye Khady, sent day and night to borrow a variety of things: some small change, a bit of dried fish, a handful of salt, just a pinch of pepper.

If the niece turned up with a bottle, it was Ousmane's job to insert the funnel in the neck of the bottle and pour in the oil or the vinegar or the bleach that she had come to 'borrow', because the Moor who kept the local shop was having his lunch or his dinner or was praying or had shut his shop.

Ousmane could never understand how his mother let herself be taken in by Auntie Kiné. That woman had the knack of never buying anything and keeping herself supplied out of Yaye Khady's stores.

She came visiting when she was sure to find Yaye Khady alone, as Djibril Gueye took a poor view of her sponging. Auntie Kiné would complain of her lot in really heartrending terms. As a third wife she had to face the united front of her co-wives, those 'old witches' who could call on a store of tricks of which she, Kiné, knew nothing.

'It's their children who torment me the worst. I don't know where to turn. They even begrudge me treading on the sand in the courtyard or breathing the air of the compound.'

Auntie Kiné deliberately exaggerated her humiliations and sufferings to touch her listeners' hearts. And Yaye Khady offered consolation, advice and loans.

Meanwhile, the boubou which her niece had taken yesterday, wrapped up in newspaper to serve as a pattern for the man who sold dress materials, was not returned.

Tomorrow, Ousmane will be sent once again to ask for it. He will find Auntie Kiné's door shut. Her niece will be sitting on the doorstep and will explain slyly, 'Auntie has gone to a baptism. She dressed herself up in a green boubou with yellow flowers and powdered her face. Auntie looks very nice in a green boubou.'

The green boubou? Ousmane's guess is that it is Yaye Khady's boubou. He will return home empty-handed. He will tell his mother, 'Auntie Kiné's not at home.'

As he's been well brought up, Ousmane wouldn't like to be known as a telltale, a mischief-maker. Yaye Khady's boubous can all make their way to Auntie Kiné's. He never let on about the use to which they were put.

Whenever Ousmane met the neighbour's niece, he would play a teasing game with her. As he walked along the street, chatting to her, he could read the adoration in the child's face. He would take the longest way home with her, holding her hand as they loitered, just to test out his powers of seduction. The child was dazzled; she was in love and would submit to all his whims.

But Ousmane had the decency not to go too far. He knew how to keep a firm hand on himself, like any respectable fellow who is aware of what he is doing. To be on the safe side he changed his route when he grew tired of these games which delighted his senses but left his heart unmoved.

So for years Ousmane seemed to have been immunised against passion. He walked through all the traps laid for him, ignoring all the meaningful glances in his direction, avoiding all the barricades set up to capture him. His heaven was darkened by clouds of mistrust.

But suddenly a bright light lit up his horizon and drove away the dark shadows. He made friends with a new pupil who joined his class — a white girl, Mireille de La Vallée, the daughter of a French diplomat. And this friendship had caused his last year at high school to pass all too quickly for his liking. They had been drawn together by their mutual interest in philosophy and their similar critical attitudes. They would prolong their critical discussions on the pavement outside the school where Mireille stood waiting for her father's car to take her home.

At the oral exam in modern languages for the Baccalauréat, Ousmane was so overcome by nerves that he forgot all his vocabulary. The answers were quite clear in his mind and he knew quite well the words needed to express them, but they persisted in eluding him. He was completely desperate. Mireille was sitting opposite him in a corner of the room where the examiner could not see her, listening to the interrogation and waiting for her turn to be 'manhandled'.

Every time Ousmane racked his treacherous memory in vain for the necessary word, Mireille would mouth it for him, and Ousmane found his bearings again and was able to get on with his exposition, his courage restored. It was as though the white girl inspired him, as if her piercing, strong-willed gaze communicated a revival of lucidity to his mind.

Noblesse oblige! as the saying goes. When it was Mireille's turn to be examined, Ousmane discreetly took her place in the same corner and came to her rescue, using the same device.

As they left the exam together they laughed mischievously at their brainwave.

When the results were announced, fortune had smiled on both of them. They had automatically passed with distinction.

They felt neither shame nor remorse. They both knew that their success was primarily dependent on their marks in the written papers.

They exchanged congratulations, comparing their answers to the different questions, picking out their respective weak points and discovering that the last question in the maths paper had been responsible for Mireille's marks being slightly lower than Ousmane's.

They parted for the holidays, quite happy, without further formality than their normal handshake and their smiles over their success.

But fate was watching over them. The first landmark on the path of their destiny had been planned.

The Ministry of Education and Culture offered Ousmane a bursary to study in France for the entrance examination to the Ecole Normale Supérieure. He chose to remain in Dakar. He had no hesitation in putting his duty to his family before his ambition and curiosity: Djibril Gueye was ageing; Yaye Khady, in her overwhelming love for her son, would scarcely get over his absence; his brothers and sisters were still young and needed his guidance.

When Ouleymatou heard of his academic success which opened up for him a future in the highest intellectual spheres, she smiled at him shyly and made opportunities to meet him, apparently by chance, in the hope of winning him over again. But Ousmane repaid her advances with an icy courtesy.

15

He could afford to be indifferent, since, when the euphoria of his success faded, he found the memory of Mireille persisting. He had imagined that his memory of her was bound up with the actual examination period. But this period gradually faded and the memory grew disproportionately stronger. The face of the white girl was always before his eyes. She mouthed the words he needed to get out of his difficulties. She shook her silky golden hair. She fluttered the long lashes over her grey-blue eyes. She smiled at him. She gazed at him.

He had only to close his eyes and hold his breath to feel the contact of her soft hand, carelessly abandoned in his, and to hear the intonations of her voice caressing his ears, beguiling him.

Ousmane found himself preferring solitude to loud discussions. To dwell on his memories and escape from the boring visits of his noisy comrades! Everything that was not associated with Mireille seemed devoid of interest. How facile Ouleymatou was, compared with his intelligent fellow-student!

The memory of her silent figure, her discreet perfume, accompanied him everywhere. This was his treasure, his secret, which he was able to bring to life at will. To him, the white girl, with her aristocratic name, was 'his princess'.

His reason, on which he had always been able to rely, told him to be on his guard against his fancy, which was shattering his vows of chastity and indifference. But Ousmane let his dream have the upper hand. He was intoxicated by his own folly.

What did it matter? He could have a little respite after the rigorous discipline involved in preparing for the exams! He could have a little respite after the exhausting efforts to avoid getting the chemical formulae mixed up! He could have a little respite and enjoy the discreet company of this invisible friend who winged her way to him so fast when he called her! He had all the more excuse for a little respite as he was certain never to see her again.

And, as never a day now passed without his dreaming of her, her quivering lips became the focal point of his desire.

4

On this first morning of the new term Ousmane arrived at the university and entered the Arts Faculty Building.

Inside everything was already in uproar. As soon as he crossed the threshold his heart leapt.

He beheld before him the gleam of a new dawn in the toss of a golden head. Suddenly the dream that he had buried in his heart and fondly caressed was coming to life. The image had stirred out of the misty recesses to which it had been confined.

That milk-white neck that Ousmane saw before him was indeed Mireille's. He had planted too many kisses on it in his dreams to be able to forget its graceful curves. He would recognise that profile even in the dark, since he had outlined it a thousand times during the three months' vacation.

And the scarcely perceptible quiver of those shimmering golden locks! The moment seemed an eternity, so deep was his emotion at the thought of this meeting. He had never imagined it to be possible and now it was a reality.

He must make a move. But how could be get going? His legs refused to obey and his pulse was racing.

'Courage!' Take it one step at a time. But every step would bring him nearer to the goal, slowly but irrevocably. He advanced. One step at a time, to be sure. But he kept going just the same.

Mireille had shrugged back her gleaming hair from her shoulders. Ousmane stretched out a hand, closed it again, then once more reached out and placed his palm with an affectionate squeeze on that patch of fair skin.

One imagines the birth of happiness to be accompanied by some great spectacular upheaval. One can imagine it flowering in the most luxurious setting. Yet happiness is born of a trifle, feeds on nothing. Enormous value is set on it. Its acquisition seems to demand a high price. Yet happiness can flourish in a university lecture theatre. A bare shoulder can bring it to life. A few steps, and it is within your grasp. A half-turned head...a face seen in profile...and fluids start to flow together to create a union. The couple is born. The first steps are taken on a thousand-year-old mission. Here, a man, a woman. Elsewhere, a man, a woman!

17

They shook hands. In the agitation and disbelief reflected in the blue eyes, Ousmane saw his own emotion mirrored. Mireille's astonishment, her obvious confusion, her blushes, gave him reason to hope that he had not been alone in hoping, in wishing. . . Had Mireille suffered the same pangs as himself? She was here. Why was she here? Perhaps — like himself — she had not been keen on France. Had she wanted to have the opportunity of seeing him again?

Now Ousmane Gueye was speaking to her. And the blue-grey eyes closed with delight. And two discreet tears ran down her blushing cheeks.

And Ousmane Gueye, who had rejected all sentimental adventures, surrendered. Ousmane Gueye, who had mistrusted all women, threw himself at the mercy of a woman, and a white woman at that. All it had needed was a handshake and a flutter of eyelashes.

Perhaps one day more imaginative lovers than Mireille and Ousmane will invent a new vocabulary and new gestures of love. Everything seemed a miracle to them, illuminated by their love. They held hands at every opportunity. They would burst out laughing at the most commonplace remarks. The hours flew past when they were together and the moments when they were apart dragged cruelly, interminably.

They were enriched by their differences. Each worried about the other over the smallest thing: a slight temperature, a scratched pimple, a bad cold. Low marks for a test, failure to understand a lecture, upset their serenity. They wanted their happiness to be perfect.

They feasted their eyes on each other. The visible parts of their bodies had no more secrets for them. When Ousmane fingered the raised scar on Mireille's forearm, she explained, 'That was a painful abscess, two years ago!' When Mireille admired her friend's sturdy build, Ousmane declared proudly, 'I've got my father's broad shoulders!'

They kissed. A kiss is the natural expression of affection. And it is the safety valve for excess desire. They would arrive early before lectures began in the morning or afternoon and take advantage of their few moments of solitude to snuggle in each other's arms. Their lips would meet and part again. They were intoxicated by this play which only ceased with the arrival of their fellow-students. They were in seventh heaven. Ousmane attended lectures without taking in a word, staring at Mireille's neck, gilded by the reflections from her hair, while she bravely took notes for both of them.

Sometimes they played truant. Across the main road, on the far side of the university, lay the sea.

As he gazed at the water, Ousmane Gueye murmured the beginning of a dictation he remembered from the primary school: 'The sea lashes the coast with its short, monotonous waves.' And Mireille added: 'And Ousmane and Mireille are in love. And Ousmane and Mireille kiss.' She suited the action to the words. They laughed, intoxicated with their youth, their illusions and the open stretch of the ocean.

They could not swim but they would throw off their shoes and paddle in the shallow water.

Sometimes they would bring a mat to lie on, and as they relaxed so their confidences would flow. There was no lack of subjects to talk about: they would report on books they had read, discuss and clarify points in their lectures, draft their essays so as to obtain the highest marks. Ousmane Gueye excelled at demonstrating how to tackle a paper.

But Ousmane never talked of himself or his family. He left Mireille the monopoly on self-revelations. She freely offered up both past and present to her sweetheart. A procession of family albums passed through Ousmane's hands, with commentaries on the photographs they contained.

'I'm an only child...You must have guessed a long time ago who my father is, from the car that you've seen him bringing me to school and university in.'

'Yes,' Ousmane replied thoughtfully. 'I'm madly in love with the daughter of a French diplomat.'

Mireille went on, 'Look at me here, with my hair tied back in a pony-tail.' Then, further on, 'Here I'm four years old. I'd just finished reading that book I'm holding. I could read when I was four. What about you?'

Without waiting for an answer she went on, 'Look at me in my ballet tutu. I had dancing lessons. Here I'm playing the piano. My parents spared no expense in making me an accomplished young lady.'

Then, pointing to a yellowing snap, 'These are my paternal grandparents. They're still alive. That's a picture of our family home at the top of the page.'

19

Ousmane observed. 'There's a river running near the house.'

'No,' Mireille corrected him. 'It's not a river; it's a lake and it's so beautiful in summer.'

As an only child, Mireille might have been very spoilt. But she had too much insight to be insolent to anyone. She would condemn rudeness as an aberration, asserting, 'There's nothing more pernicious.' The source of her unfailing courtesy was her belief in the equality of all mankind, reinforced by the good manners that she had been taught.

She added, 'Contrary to the usual custom, ever since I've been old enough, I've been the one to go to my parents' bedroom and kiss them goodnight.'

Ousmane listened. His pride and self-respect would not allow him to speak of the working-class neighbourhood of Usine Niari Talli. He erected a mental barrier between the aristocratic Mireille and the red earth walls of his parents' hut. He said aloud, 'I will never speak of my family or let you into the secret garden of my origins until I am ready to ask you to be my wife.'

Mireille never pressed him, respecting his reserve. Ousmane's silence only added to the mystery of their love.

Ousmane speculated. 'Do you really love me? Don't you think of me as the one rare toy missing from your collection, in your world where your every wish is gratified?'

Mireille simply tossed her mane of fair hair by way of reply. She believed in a love that knew no national frontiers. What she looked for in a partner was intelligence and charm: Ousmane was one of the brightest in their class; and he was good-looking — as handsome as a statue. 'You've got extraordinarily fine features,' she told him, 'they might have been modelled by a sculptor.'

Mireille was genuinely in love. She did not lie to him. Her French parents' upper-middle-class conservatism was powerless in the face of the laws of attraction which drew her to Ousmane. This was not a deliberate reaction to having been born with a silver spoon in her mouth. She had no psychological trauma to counteract; she did not feel the need to fill any gap in her life; she had no grudge to satisfy, no physical or moral blemish to compensate for, nothing to rebel against, no yoke to break. She was simply and naturally in love, like any healthy, normal girl of her age.

'I can't explain my feelings. Why should it have to be you?' she often used to say with a laugh.

And it was because she was in love that she had experienced that spontaneous, irrepressible desire to help him when she had seen him in difficulties at the exam. It was that maternal, protective instinct which lies buried in every woman in love.

During the whole holidays she had thought of nothing but Ousmane, and how she could see him again. She had taken a risk, like a person in a fire who throws herself out of a window.

Her registration at the university was no coincidence. She had had to fight to get her way. Her parents owned a luxury flat in Paris, and the elderly maiden aunt who occupied it would have been delighted to have Mireille living with her.

'Who can resist love pleading its cause?' Mireille asked mischievously.

She had expected to have the utmost difficulty in tracking Ousmane down. And it had been so simple! Here they were together and she could run her finger round the perfect oval of Ousmane's face, pat his cheeks and admire that fine torso that she had last glimpsed a few months ago.

In the face of so much devotion, Ousmane might one day be prepared to describe his wash-room built of old, leaking sheets of galvanised iron; he might mention Djibril's shortened leg, introduce Yaye Khady's charming smile, regardless of the flower gardens, the comfortable furniture, the fitted kitchens, the profusion of toys and clothes, the bookshelves filled with leather-bound volumes seen in the background of the photographs in the albums they had pored over together.

The most recent photograph in one of the albums showed Mireille in a long blue dress with a white flower on her left shoulder, standing in the vast drawing-room of the diplomatic residence.

Their childhoods had nothing in common. Ousmane's hands had been calloused by wielding the short broom; he had been drenched by the water that splashed out of the buckets he carried.

Was he a possible partner for Mireille? Could he assume such a mutation?

He was poor, it is true. But poverty is not an infirmity. Neither is it a criterion for respectability.

How do you judge a person's superiority? A man's greatness? Surely by his intelligence, his heart, his virtues!

And, as far as these were concerned, Ousmane felt himself to be a Man, worthy of every manifestation of love.

Mireille easily wiped out any lingering memory of Ouleymatou. She was the antidote to the poison in Ousmane's heart; she restored his confidence; she overcame his defences. She took victorious possession of a heart that was fancy-free and a body that had kept itself available for love.

The months flew past, driven on by Time, the shepherd.

In Ousmane Gueye's dreams, his love gave him the strength to move mountains, to demolish the many obstacles in the way of a permanent union with his beloved. In Ousmane's dreams Mireille coquettishly swirled her full skirts or strutted in tight-fitting jeans. She loosened her shining hair for her sweetheart to rumple fondly.

They exchanged photographs to appease their impatience for each other when they were apart. Mireille's picture, encased in a wrought iron frame, behind glass, enjoyed a place of honour on Ousmane's work table in his tiny room.

One day Yaye Khady's clumsy little maid knocked the photograph over while she was tidying the books. The glass broke. When Ousmane saw the damage he flew into a terrible rage which nobody could understand. He fell on his knees, picking the splintered glass from the picture and feverishly stroking the figure in the frame. His features were distorted by the intensity of his emotion, and this attitude of reverence astonished Yaye Khady.

Again he began to stroke the portrait, saying aloud, 'Fortunately the picture didn't get scratched!'

Yaye Khady, more and more astonished, retorted, 'And what if it had been? You should just see yourself trembling over the picture of a film-star you don't even know! Fancy being so much at the mercy of a myth!'

To dispel his mother's anxiety, Ousmane joked, 'Yes, and *you* get even more worked up over the wrestler Doudou Ndoye. You do nothing but sing about his exploits day in day out. Is my father shocked?'

They laughed and the incident was forgotten. Ousmane obtained a new glass and the photograph was replaced in its frame.

Mireille did not frame Ousmane's photograph and it had no fixed place in her room. At night she kept it under her pillow and every morning slipped it into her dressing-gown pocket. Then she moved it into one of her files or between the pages of a book, according to what she was working on at the time.

But the portrait accompanied every action of her daily life. When she went to take a shower, she placed it in a corner of the bathroom and smiled at it. She took it to bed with her and kissed it goodnight. When she got into the car to drive to the university, she held it in her hand to protect it from the jolts.

She had chosen this snap from the dozens she had taken of Ousmane. 'That one's come off! It's a really good likeness!' Her sweetheart was standing on a black rock, round which a very blue sea washed. His red shirt was open to the waist, revealing a fine chain that Mireille had given him hanging from his neck. He was smiling broadly, showing his regular teeth. His eyes shone with mischief and intelligence.

At night the photo reminded her of the pleasures they had shared. Their association, recent as it was, already had its share of memories: there had been fits of the sulks, after which they had rushed to make it up; there had been times when their passion could barely be restrained; the winding path they had travelled together was already beset with lurking dangers.

But one day Mireille mislaid the snapshot. No more blue sea, no more black rock, red shirt, white-toothed smile, shining eyes. She searched in vain for the precious object. She ransacked her wardrobe, turned out her drawers, but it did not come to light. She swept under the bed and turned over the mattress without result and with increasing anxiety. Her mother might have helped her, but she would have to know what was causing her child so much agitation and worry.

Mireille was tormented by the thought that her father might find the photo. She dreaded the 'dialogue' that would ensue. Her cheeks grew scarlet at the thought. Ousmane noticed her anxiety. She had to confess that the snapshot had disappeared, explaining how she had looked everywhere and what she feared. 'Now you'll have to be satisfied to have my picture in here,' Ousmane consoled her, tapping her forehead.

Over the years since Mireille's father had been posted to Senegal, the household had known that calm associated with a rigid, unshakable routine.

Mireille always woke early. She brought her parents their breakfast in bed — a task she had assumed as soon as she was old enough to manage the taps on the gas-stove.

A tray of coffee, croissants and jam for her father; tea for her mother without any bread or butter. Madame de la Vallée kept her appetite well under control with a strict diet. In this way she fought against a tendency to put on weight, as her husband's position demanded that she retain her beauty and poise.

Mireille would kiss her parents and set her watch by their alarm clock. She would sit on one of the twin beds and they would chat over this and that — serious problems or trifles — exchange confidences, discuss the news, mention jobs to be done, invitations to be accepted or hospitality to be reciprocated, the programme for the day's activities.

Mireille would then leave her parents to their breakfast trays. She would rush off to her bath to be in time for the keep-fit programme on the radio. She now had an extra reason — a lover in her life — to retain a supple, graceful body.

Then came the important choice of what clothes to wear. How should she look today for Ousmane? The instinctive desire of a woman in love was to look her most beguiling. She wanted to ring the changes daily on her appearance. She spent her allowance on toiletries and make-up which she used discreetly to enhance the sheen of her hair or add a touch of colour to her lips and cheeks. She gave off a faint aroma of eau de cologne.

Yesterday she had looked sensational in her white shirt and trousers with a turquoise scarf. The previous day, a very full green dress with matching shoes had set off the colour of her eyes.

Today? She flicked through hanger after hanger in her wardrobe. Nothing seemed appropriate, nothing able to bewitch Ousmane. Finally she decided on a red print dress with a pattern of tiny leaves that her paternal grandmother had recently sent her.

'Will Ousmane be wearing his red shirt?' she wondered. 'The one in the snapshot? Then our clothes would match...'

The thought of the little photo revived her anxiety, added to the fact that she could hear her father beginning his day with a noisy and energetic bath.

Her mother was talking to the servants, giving them instructions for the day's work.

Mireille raced downstairs, fresh and sweet-scented. The car door slammed. The chauffeur speeded off towards the university, slowing down in front of the Le Dantec Hospital, where crowds of out-patients overflowed into the middle of the road.

5

That evening saw a disruption in the calm and uneventful routine of the diplomatic residence.

Mireille came home from her lectures at six o'clock, after spending a little time agreeably with her boy-friend. She hummed to herself as she climbed the stairs.

'Mireille!'

Her father's grim voice bellowed out from the sitting room which was plunged in darkness with the curtains drawn. She went back downstairs.

She glimpsed her mother sitting stiffly, scarcely recognisable. A huge ashtray placed between her parents was overflowing with half-smoked cigarettes.

The photograph! They had discovered her secret! Ousmane was delivered over in his red shirt to her parents' anger! His bared chest was at the mercy of their contempt! She put on a brave face and advanced slowly into the room. She went over to her father and bent down to kiss him as usual but he turned his head away and her lips met his chin in a harsh rebuff. She did not dare embrace her mother whose tense attitude forbade any approach.

Jean de la Vallée took the snapshot out of an envelope. Mireille suffered to see how creased and stained it was. The surface was scratched as if it had been attacked by somone's nails. 'While it was in my possession,' Mireille thought, 'that picture was treated with care and respect.'

'Do you recognise this object?' her father launched at her. And without waiting for an answer he went on scornfully, 'Of course you recognise it. It's inscribed, "To my beloved Mireille, Ousmane".' He held out the picture contemptuously in the tips of his fingers, as if it was contaminated.

Her mother sat looking down throughout this confrontation. Her white blouse accentuated the pallor of her face and neck. Her hands, resting in her lap, trembled nervously. Mireille proudly took 'that object'. The picture that she knew so well, that she had studied in every light, seemed to live again as it had done so recently, when she smiled at it, assuring it of her affection, her hopes, her plans.

'This object' was important in her life. 'This object' was her happiness. Ousmane was present, living in 'this object'. Once more their understanding filled her with gentle warmth. Once more she was under the spell of love, fired by the finely chiselled features, the bared chest, the red shirt, the blue sky, the black rock, the sun that shone out of his eyes.

Ousmane seemed alive. Ousmane was embracing her. One scene stood out vividly in her memory, the most meaningful of all the scenes that she relived. They were accustomed to meet, either in the company of other students, or just the two of them alone, according to the day, in the room at the University Residence of a friend of Ousmane's called Ali.

They had given to this room the grand name of *Keur Ali*, 'The Abode of Ali', and there they spent their leisure moments listening to records or just chatting. In *Keur Ali* the sweethearts were safe from discovery. But the rare occasions when they could be alone there and the precautions they had to take to protect the slender thread of their happiness, tinged their meetings with sadness.

One evening, in an effort to throw off some rather persistent fellow-students, Ousmane had pretended to be leaving. Then, when he had got rid of his indiscreet companions, he retraced his steps.

He found Mireille alone, reclining on the only bed, her profusion of hair loose about her head, her bare legs stretched out in graceful symmetry, her fine eyes half-closed in the suspense of waiting.

Ousmane stroked her forehead, her long golden hair. His hands played over her cool body. He buried his burning lips in the soft places of her fresh young skin.

As the light faded, they could scarcely see their bodies. They embraced more passionately than usual. Ousmane held Mireille tight to himself. He clasped her supple young form powerfully and she abandoned herself, obedient to his desires.

The girl felt an agonising pain pierce to her very womb. The hoarse moan that lingered on her parted lips brought Ousmane to his senses. But her cry had been followed by an overwhelming ecstasy that invaded her whole being. Mireille's cheeks were bathed in tears. Ousmane was perspiring.

He fell on his knees and begged her to forgive him. But his body that had had its way vibrated with rapture. His shining eyes belied his words of regret. Their faces met, mingling tears of happiness and reconciliation.

Faced with her parents' demands for her to repent and repudiate her friend, Mireille relived this scene. She had given her heart and also her body. The irrevocable had been achieved.

Tears, yes! But no regrets! Still more tears, but she wept because of her love, because she was like the ivy found in her country, which when it chose to cling could never be dislodged. Her heart was now inseparable from the one to whom she had given her body.

She stammered out, 'Yes, I know him. He's very intelligent. You should get to know him before you pass judgement.'

She would have continued pleading her case — for hours? for months? — to no avail, for judgement had already been passed on her and her sentence allowed no appeal.

A resounding blow stung her face! She choked on the words she was about to utter. She just had time to see her mother collapse on the floor as she fled out of the room, sobbing loud and desperately, and took refuge in her own bedroom.

She was not surprised by her father's violence. It allowed her to measure her own folly, the extent of this madness that had taken complete possession of her. An exhilarating madness. She would not give it up. On the contrary, she had a thousand reasons to sing it from the rooftops. All she wanted was to be happy with Ousmane. She swore to stand her ground.

The morning after this violent scene Mireille woke early as usual, in spite of her reddened eyes, her dry throat and fevered brow; her lips were swollen from the blow she had received and her head ached from turning over possible solutions, to be rejected one after another, as each appeared more unreasonable than the last. From force of habit she prepared the two breakfast trays—and found herself up against a locked door.

She bathed quickly, dressed in the first outfit to hand and hid her tear-stained eyes behind dark glasses. She covered the cut on her face with a piece of sticking plaster.

She was about to make her way downstairs, where the chauffeur was waiting for her as usual, when her father, recognising her step, burst out of his bedroom and barred her way.

'No more university! I realise now: it's because of that nigger that you wanted to stay on here. I don't want any scandal. You don't realise how serious your behaviour is, in view of my position.'

Mireille fell back, horrified. She was staggered at her father's language. Was this the same man who made speeches preaching fraternisation with the indigenous peoples?

Her father's voice echoed other voices heard in the course of receptions and meetings, those of his compatriots who were past-masters at the art of denigration and ridicule. African chiefs were their favourite targets. They contrived to pick out the weaknesses and errors of their behaviour in snide remarks, pregnant with hints and nudges. Her father remained silent and aloof during these mud-slinging sessions. For that reason she believed in the possibility of her dream.

And now her eyes were suddenly opened. Her father, always so restrained in voice and attitude, had been making every effort to keep a firm hold on the violence that risked being aroused by his aversion to the Black. That violence was now out of control. Mireille recoiled, horrified.

Her father was now making no secret of the disgust her friend inspired. In what way was the latter's father inferior to her own father? One day, overcoming the rigid reticence he always observed about his parents, Ousmane had told her that his father had been wounded in the war and that was why he could claim a pension.

Detesting ingratitude and upheld by a sincere belief in the equality of all men, Mireille turned to confront her father with the courage of her convictions. Stinging words tumbled from her lips.

'The father of ''that object'' as you call him, fought for our country at the risk of his life. He's disabled from the wound he received, a victim of somebody else's cause. Ousmane's father defended our history and protected our safety. What have you done for him in return? Your presence here? That's not out of any altruism. You're in the service of your own country, like an unarmed soldier in civilian garb keeping a watchful eye on someone else's business. You're still the same old coloniser, just disguised as a humanitarian, still playing your own game, which is simply and solely to exploit this country. But I'm not playing your game; I'm on the other side, and I'm not going back on that, you understand . . .'

Nothing could stop Mireille now. 'Ousmane is part of me,' she went on. 'I have heard his heart beat. Beause of him and his fine qualities I have rejected all those old assumptions that are drummed into us by racist anecdotes: the grinning primitive Negro of the ''Banania'' adverts; the educationally sub-normal Negro; the pudgy-faced, round-eyed Negro! I'll take them all on! You think you're superior because you're white. But just scratch yourself. You'll bleed the same red blood, a sign that you're the same as all people on earth. Your heart isn't on the right. It's on the left, Daddy, the same as every human heart. You've got a brain and a liver which do the same job as Ousmane's brain and liver. Tell me, in what way are you any better? Why did you give in when I expressed the wish to study here? To please me, to be sure, but also to enhance your own image. It looks good—a diplomat's daughter attending the university in the country where he's posted. It shows his ''liberal ideas'', his ''progressive tendencies''—so many big-sounding phrases that cover up real petty prejudices. You've shaken my confidence and destroyed the illusions prompted by my affection for you. I'm in love, do you understand! I love a black man, a man black as coal. Black! Black! I love this man and I won't give him up simply because he's black!'

This was the impassioned, unequivocal voice of love, railing at all the so-called truths with which the girl had been indoctrinated. Monsieur de La Vallée was helpless in the face of the age-old torrents of unleashed passion. Taken completely by surprise by the unexpected vehemence of her language, he clenched his fists tightly to help control his anger. He snapped, 'You're a minor! A minor! Good God, you're not old enough to understand! It's my job to protect you. And I will protect you, in spite of yourself! I'm packing you off home this evening.'

He turned on his heels. Mireille screamed after him, 'Don't count on my killing myself. From now on, every beat of my heart will bring me nearer to Ousmane. Ousmane! You understand? Ousmane!'

She rushed back to her room and threw herself headlong on to the bed. As she grew calmer she tried to put her ideas into some order . . .

Her thoughts turned fondly to her mother. She telephoned through to her room and asked if she could see her. Her mother refused to answer. The servant told her that Madam was very poorly. 'The doctor has been three times since yesterday.'

'She's suffered a severe shock.' Mireille acknowledged.

Her parents' reaction did not surprise her. The realities of life only reached that bourgeois elite filtered and categorised. The heritage of what it was correct to do and think had its taboos and

29

forbidden areas. Between preaching the equality of all men and practising it there was an abyss fraught with peril, and they were not equipped to make this leap.

Beneath the crystal chandeliers of the drawing-rooms they frequented, they shook black hands with a smile on their lips but no warmth in their hearts.

Sadly Mireille tossed back her hair. She had been caught unprepared and had no idea what to do next. How was she to let Ousmane know what had happened? He would be sick with worry until she could explain everything to him. It would be too risky to ask the servant or the chauffeur to take a message: if they were found out they would be dismissed on the spot.

She tore at the sheets in her frustration. In her fury she buried her head in the pillow, ran her hands through her hair, stamped her feet. She screamed and wept in a flood of misery and pain. She hammered on the door with her fists.

She was still sobbing when a servant brought two empty suit-cases which he put down on the floor.

'The master told me to bring these for you to do your packing, Miss Mireille.'

So her father was carrying out his threat to send her home without delay.

'What difference does it make!' When food was sent up to her at meal-times she refused to eat.

'What difference does it make!' She shoved clothes, books, toiletries any old how into the two cases. But she carefully sorted all the letters she had received from her sweetheart and tied them in a neat packet into which she slipped the snapshot which she had retrieved.

She waited for it to be time to leave. Her father had sent word by the servant that she should be ready at ten o'clock.

It was already quite dark, with irregular streaks of light suspended between earth and sky, as the diplomatic car drove past the National Assembly and along the corniche in the direction of Yoff Airport.

Mireille shivered as she passed this way once more. The car speeded past the university. On the left, behind these rocks, lay 'her beach'. The sound of the waves breaking was torment to her wounded heart!

She sat huddled in the back seat, her eyes brimming with tears.

The village of Ouakam. A steep climb. A precautionary stop.

In front, the beam from the Almadies lighthouse swept across the night sky. A sharp turn. The Ngor hotel shone out of the darkness, like a lantern spangled with little stars. Luxurious cars were drawn up in front of the Cape Verde Casino.

An ominous silence separated father and daughter as the car thrust back the darkness. From time to time a necessary gear change, a sudden jolt. The car finally drew up in front of the VIP parking of the airport.

Mireille did not wait for her father's permission to alight. She made for the concourse and sat down. Monsieur de La Vallée saw to the embarkation formalities and the registration of the two suitcases.

The whole airport was abustle. The Minister of Foreign Affairs was expected back from a long mission through Africa and members of the cabinet, friends, relatives and electors, hoping for a quiet word in his ear, waited impatiently to greet him, drinking fruit-juice to while away the time. This party's noisy good humour, their loud laughter and complacent attitudes set Mireille's nerves on edge.

People who recognised Monsieur de La Vallée greeted him respectfully. Relaxed, affable, smiling, the diplomat cordially took outstretched black hands. He shook his head: 'No, I'm not leaving. I'm seeing my daughter off. She's rather run down and is off to get some mountain air. A breath of fresh air is always good when one is growing.'

And he pointed with an expression of concern to where Mireille sat, huddled in her pullovers, fearing for her future. Her reddened eyes and drawn features could well be interpreted as signs of illness. The diplomat, well versed in the arts of correct behaviour, was playing the part of the anxious father to perfection, masking the real cause of his mental torment. Not a trace of racist indignation in his voice or manner. Reproaches? Forgotten! Threats? Vanished!

The pleasant, neutral voice of the air hostess came over the loud-speaker, requesting passengers to board the aircraft.

The diplomat smiled, cordially shook black hands again by way of leave-taking and affectionately guided his daughter towards the departure gate. The gangway was already in place and the first passengers were boarding.

He gave Mireille the kiss he had refused yesterday and she returned his greeting passively, like a mummy.

She walked up the gangway and flopped, exhausted, into the first

31

vacant seat, draping her crumpled pullovers over her legs. She put the back of her seat into the upright position and fastened her seat-belt without waiting for the hostess's announcement.

The engines throbbed. The plane rose from the ground, high into the air.

Mireille was lost in her own thoughts. The stewardess passed back and forth, smiling at her each time, guessing that this girl, travelling alone in the first class, must be the diplomat's daughter on whom she had been asked to keep a discreet eye.

Mireille did not respond to the stewardess's friendly overtures. She refused refreshments and reading matter. Gradually she fell asleep, overcome by fatigue.

The unpleasant biting cold which greeted Mireille revived her pain.

She was flung into a change of country, university, the framework of her life, without making any attempt to re-adapt. With disgust, she recognised in everything her father's methods: strictness and efficiency personified, without the slightest trace of sentiment.

Orders had been given, acquaintances made use of, to make sure that she lacked for nothing.

But how did they hope that the change of country would influence her? That the separation would make her forget her love? On the contrary, the sharp cold only made her long the more for the warm sun.

No sooner had she arrived than she dashed off a letter to Ousmane, to re-establish the link that had been so cruelly broken.

She slipped into a large envelope the last photograph from her album, the one where she was wearing the long blue dress, adorned with a white rose.

She re-read her letter, folded it carefully and put it in the envelope with the photograph.

6

Ousmane received, via the university administration, a large pink envelope, covered with foreign stamps.

Mireille's handwriting! Handwriting free of flourishes that denoted the writer's determined character. He was as wildly excited as when he had recognised the back of Mireille's neck, her bare shoulder and her hair, on the day the new university year began.

Dare he be overjoyed? The pink colour of the envelope inspired optimism. But the girl's sudden return to France augured no good as far as her relationship with her parents was concerned. If the journey had been prepared in advance she would have let him know. But she had disappeared without warning.

His enquiries over the past four days had met with an impenetrable wall of silence. Tormented by anxiety, he had ventured into the precincts of the diplomatic residence. But the buildings, surrounded by a vast garden, betrayed no secret.

Yaye Khady noted with despair her son's irritability and withdrawal. She had an intuitive feeling that some important event had occurred in her child's life but all her feminine wiles could not discover anything.

Now Ousmane never left his work-table. He sat staring at Mireille's photograph, to drown his senses in the image of his beloved. He pretended to be studying, sitting with an open book in front of him, his elbows planted on the table, but with her face in his hands. His whole being, at these moments, was drawn to his absent sweetheart.

The envelope which he now held would either relieve his anxiety or intensify it. The letter quivered in his hand, the bearer of a message, like an envoy of fate.

He could not wait to find out its contents. 'Too bad about Prof. Sy's lecture. He'll have to hold forth without me.' He slipped discreetly out of the lecture room.

He had to read Mireille's letter in the presence of her photograph, with the complicity of his own little room, which had witnessed his cries of despair in the night, when overcome with longing for her.

Now he would not heed the street's invitation to listen and look about him. The bond that had grown up between them from their long-standing communion, had weakened with the presence of Mireille in his life. 'Let the street sulk,' he thought, 'or shout out my ingratitude if it likes!' And he hailed a taxi.

'Usine Niari Talli,' he directed. 'As fast as you can.'

The Ouakam road, Point E, Zones Z and B, district by district swallowed up by the taxi's wheels.

'Faster! Faster!' Ousmane pleaded.

He brought the wild ride to a halt a hundred metres from his house, so as not to alarm his mother who had never seen him arrive by taxi.

Nevertheless Yaye Khady expressed her astonishment.

'Back already! On a Monday! Are you ill?'

'No. It's the Professor who's unwell.'

Yaye Khady muttered her disapproval. 'But when that happens you usually stay and work in the library.'

In spite of his irritation at this discussion, Ousmane answered lightly, 'No library today! I'm taking the morning off to rest.'

This was an excuse to bolt his door and close the shutters. But he lit the lamp which gave him away.

'He's lit the lamp. So he's not sleeping. What sort of a rest is this?' Yaye Khady wondered.

A vague maternal instinct told her that her Oussou was growing up. He doubtless had a secret. A woman he was worried about? It must be a woman! Only love can be the cause of irrational behaviour: you don't put on the light when you want to rest. Ousmane was in love. Perhaps he was unhappy!

She was pleased with her deduction, for she feared lest her son live up to his nickname of 'the Priest' and remain celibate.

The curiosity that tortured her tempted her to peer through a couple of cracks in the wooden walls of the hut.

She restrained herself. 'Suppose Ousmane caught me spying on him? . . .'

And her dignity prevented her giving way to the temptation.

She found an outlet for her restlessness in returning to the preparation of the midday meal, peeling and scraping the vegetables with more than usual care and dropping them into a calabash of water.

In his locked room Ousmane undressed as if preparing for battle. He was indeed engaged in a battle, which was no less hard for not requiring physical strength. He foresaw a bitter struggle for which

34

Mireille was the prize. His sweetheart's parents were armed with solid arguments. If they could convince Mireille, he would be the loser. He would be cast aside like a wisp of straw, his illusions shattered as they had been with Ouleymatou.

And suppose Mireille chose him instead of wealth and the easy life? Suppose Mireille chose the black son of a disabled ex-serviceman and an illiterate housewife?

If Mireille chose him, the prophecies of his mother's friends would be fulfilled. They had predicted, 'When a son is devoted to his parents, there will always be room for him at the top'. And he had passed his matric.

They had predicted, 'When a boy has no complexes about helping his mother (they knew all the menial jobs about the house Ousmane had taken on as a boy), God raises him up in return to undreamed-of moral and material heights and smoothes all the difficulties in his path.'

With tears in her eyes Yaye Khady had said 'Amen to that!'

'That's enough of these disgressions,' Ousmane said to himself and finally opened the envelope. A photograph which he recognised fell out. He picked it up, gazed at it, kissed it. The photograph raised his hopes.

He smiled at the neat, legible handwriting. The resolute words, the expression of heart-felt but diffident affection, were characteristic of Mireille, whose distant voice now spoke so lovingly in his ear.

This was her declaration:

'Ousmane,

We shan't be able to hug and kiss any more before lectures. We shan't be able to bunk boring old Prof. Sy's classes, leaving him to drone on while we enjoy the sea air nearby. Not that I have stopped loving you.

Because I refuse to give you up I have been sent back home like an exile.

The little snapshot of you was found in my father's car and provoked a showdown.

How right you were when you drew my attention to the Wolof proverb: ''What one does not know does not exist.''

My parents would have got to know somehow, through the photograph or some other means. The fact that they know about you frees me from anxiety from the need to be always on my guard and, above all, from the need to lie.

The most important thing for me is to know where you stand. I know nothing whatever about you. I don't know who you are, except as far as we are concerned, as a couple.

35

I'm not asking you for anything you don't want to tell me. But in order to fight, I must know what I am fighting for.

If I must give you up, say so without embarrassment. You have given me such wonderful happiness that I am ready to forgive you anything. If you love me enough to wish to build a future with me, then I am ready. If, when my present misery and solitude come to an end, I find you waiting for me with open arms, everything will seem easy. But we shall have to wait four years, till I am legally of age.

Just tell me what to do and nothing else except you will matter.

Write to me. I shall be waiting.

Mireille.

There followed a girl-friend's box number, to which he could address his reply.

Ousmane re-read the sentence: 'Just tell me what to do and nothing else will matter!'

The letter meant that he now had to give serious thought to his position, that he had to make a choice between two irreconcilable decisions, which either way would bring heartache. Ousmane compared himself to the hero of a Corneille drama. 'On the one side, my heart draws me to a white girl . . . on the other, my own people. My reason fluctuates between the two, like the arm of a balance on which two objects of equal value are weighed.'

Reject the Usine Niari Talli district? Escape from its clutches? Spew up its stench? It was tempting! But his home kept a tight grip on him. These loud voices in his ear, singing in unison of traditional values, urging obedience to the dictates of a collective existence, these were the voices of his birthplace. Any departure from the norm, any violent change was a source of bewilderment, derision or indignation. The torch of his cultural heritage lighting up the only path for him to follow . . . Minds fossilised by the antiquated ideas of the past . . . Protected by their armour-plating, manners and customs were safe against attack . . .

MBowène! MBoupène! Thiamène! Shoemakers—musicians and praise-singers—jewellers! Trades and crafts handed down from father to son since time immemorial and granted their own compounds . . . Religion, teaching tolerance, remaining the indestructible link between them all . . .

Usine Niari Talli enfolded him. Yaye Khady's love was echoed in the hearts of all the women of the neighbourhood, all mothers by proxy, ready to wipe his chronically running nose, surrogate mothers, always watching over him, never hesitating to punish him when he rummaged in rubbish heaps for junk, bits of salvage, empty cans, cardboard boxes that his child's imagination transformed into matchless toys . . . Were he to fall ill, the whole neighbourhood would ask anxiously after him. Every hand would bring talismans and holy water to deliver him from the spells of some invisible sorcerer. He remembered tossing and shivering with fever and throbbing temples, during a severe attack of malaria, while to his anxious ears came murmured advice on the ingredients, which invariably included garlic, for a rub-down with miraculuous powers . . .

Usine Niari Talli would not easily accept defeat; the area was an education in itself, a fount of enrichment, the crucible of inviolable traditions from which the heart and the soul drew their strength.

Generous in their poverty, discreet in their tribulations, respectable in their wretchedness, tolerant in their differences—such were the inhabitants of his neighbourhood.

Was he to reject Usine Niari Talli? Curse the early-morning din of hooting cars and screeching tyres? His mental anguish seemed reflected in the glowing coals of the braziers. Out of the past came the memory of bowling happily along after old abandoned tyres. Once again he relived the scrum and the chase after an old burst football, till he and his pals dropped from exhaustion . . .

Was he to reject Usine Niari Talli? No longer heed the pointing finger of his father's respected fellow Muslims, directing him towards God's royal road? Never more be moved to meditation at the sound of the muezzin, under the minaret of a mosque bathed in the purple glow of dawn? Shred the thousand pages of his ancestral heritage? Trample underfoot the talismans that protected him and his people? Repudiate the *rabs* and the jinnee? Divert from its proper channel the blood which is the carrier of virtues? Decry pride in one's birth? Die for love and not for honour? Would he dare take this step? He made a supreme effort to disengage himself. But was it easy to break loose from the ties that bound him to his native baobabs? Would he dare take this step? The angry faces of the dead glowered contemptuously. Their memory protested. The thunder of vengeance growled. Would he dare? To choose a wife outside the community was an act of treason and he had been taught, 'God punishes traitors'. There was the warning axiom,

37

'Dérétou Tegal dou moye lou pou borom!' (The blood of the circumcision flows only onto one's own thigh.)

He shivered with foreboding. Tentacles held him in their crushing grip. The more he strove to break free the tighter the coils enfolded him. How could he escape without amputating a part of himself? How could he escape without bleeding to death?

But his heart leapt. Mireille, radiant in her photographs, held out her invitation. He shook his head . . . 'On the one side, Mireille . . . On the other, my people . . . My parents . . .

'My parents? Their reaction will be as hostile as that of Mireille's parents.' They would express the same horror and disgust at what the stranger would bring into their midst. It is true that Djibril Gueye had had experience of white folk. But he had never forgotten that he was different from them, and he was proud of that difference. How could he widen his father's horizon? By what means could he jolt his conscience to the acceptance of a new order? How could he prove to him that there were other truths?

A sneeze from Yaye Khady reminded him of her presence. 'Yaye Khady is possessive! Pig-headed. How could I win her over? Yaye Khady will fight tenaciously. Yaye Khady will fight . . . to her last breath . . .' Ousmane admitted to himself.

He also admitted, 'In Usine Niari Talli I shall be a *guena het* . . . a traitor to my people . . . whose behaviour will be denounced and held up as a warning. As for my friends . . .'

His friends had seen what they thought was simply a passing infatuation develop into a passion. They had expressed their disapproval without mincing their words. The bearded member of the group had warned him, 'No, no and no again! The reign of mixed marriages is over. That type of marriage was acceptable during the colonial period, when blacks on the make could get promotion and profit from marriage to a white woman. But a man should look for a wife among his own people. These whites are racists. Their former humanitarianism was nothing but a snare, a shameful weapon of exploitation to lull our consciences. But in their own country there's no equivocation! No mask! Taxi drivers refuse black passengers. Doudou told us that to reserve a room in a hotel you have to phone up . . . "Yes, there's a room available . . . immediately!" And as soon as you let on you are black, the available room has disappeared.'

Boly, the guitarist, had insisted, 'Outside your physical relationship, what will you and your white woman have in common? You can't build a future without a shared past. So many mixed marriages are crushed by misunderstandings. Africa can be cruel in her jealousy. So look out!'

Arguments and more arguments!

But Love gradually overcame them. Ousmane pleaded with himself.

'One must take risks. Progress demands changing the way people think. Life requires taking risks. There's no reason why I should fail, simply because other people have not succeeded. How many marriages break down throughout the world? But people still go on getting married. Mireille is not the sort to act on a whim. She is not a starry-eyed romantic out for exotic adventures. She is in love. I must live my own life! I must build my own future instead of letting others choose for me.'

'That'll be difficult,' retorted Reason. 'Difficult in your present situation. Difficult with a mother like yours!'

But Love insisted, 'All you'll have to do, is to put your life as Mireille's husband in one compartment, and that as Yaye Khady's son, the son of Niari Talli in another.'

And Love added further advice, 'Don't give in without a fight. Success is possible.'

Ousmane continued to ponder. He would write that evening.

But before entering into any engagement, he would make it quite clear he would never renounce his black identity. He would make it a condition that Mireille should first convert to Islam. Brought up in the path of Allah, a convinced and practising Muslim, following in the footsteps of a father who was a former *talibé*, Ousmane could not conceive of marriage except in the mosque. He would state this categorically.

'I will never split myself apart for you. I will never lose my identity for you!' Ousmane reflected.

He would write straight away, that very evening. Before entering into any engagement he would tell her of the unquestionable position of Yaye Khady and Djibril Gueye; he would describe his shack standing amid nauseous effluvia from stopped-up drains. He would present his little den with its dozens of chinks in its wooden walls.

Safiétou, toddling around with her bare bottom, amulets festooning her legs, snot dripping from her nose, would bob respectfully to Mireille. His sweetheart's delicate nostrils would be assailed by the odour of dried fish that clung to the neighbourhood.

But he would also write of his love. He would describe his solitude and his suffering and the emptiness of his days and nights! How much he too would be suffering from his 'exile in his own country'!

He composed in his head the sentences he would use, gesticulating as he rejected an unsuitable word, rubbing it out in his mind, starting over again. He hopped about. Happiness stimulated his reflexes and buried his scruples.

Yaye Khady listened. She fancied she could hear him dancing.

Mad with joy, Ousmane threw himself down on his mattress of dried moss. He sighed deeply and loud with relief, now that his anxieties were over. He was about to enter on a new phase of his life!

Yaye Khady listened. She smiled. The sound advised her of her son's victory. She was unaware of the nature of his struggle. But what matter! That sigh indicated a victory! Her son! Her Oussou!

She rose to her feet humming. She shook off the vegetable peels that clung to her pagne. She walked over to the cooking-pot balanced on three large stones over a wood fire. She raised the lid, holding it with a piece of paper, dipped her right index finger in the sauce to check the seasoning.

She continued to martyrise the vegetables, savaging them with her sharp knife: the boiling water swallowed them up.

At lunchtime, when Ousmane unbolted his door, Yaye Khady caught sight of another picture of his film-star, in another pose, beside the first wrought-iron frame.

She teased him, 'Put that she-devil that you're so besotted with in a frame, or I won't answer for her presence!'

Ousmane was only too happy to comply.

Yaye Khady suspected nothing, any more than Djibril Gueye did.

7

May 1968 found the de La Vallée family back in Paris. This was a period when Mireille was a prey to attacks of depression. She was consumed with desire, which her loneliness only intensified. All her energies seemed to have dried up.

How she would have loved to throw off her reserve, her polite behaviour, her daily calm, and express her inner disquiet.

She had agreed to all Ousmane's uncompromising demands. She was not disheartened by the difficulties of their venture, which he laid relentlessly before her. He did his best to discourage her. 'Don't let your choice settle on me!' he admonished her. 'There's still time to change your mind!' But these exhortations did not deter Mireille from standing by her decision.

The religion she had promised to discard had long ill-suited her. As she grew older, so she had outgrown its many prohibitions. She wrote back to him, *'The religion that you wish me to adopt is neither more nor less suited to me than the one you ask me to abandon. But I will accept it . . . without enthusiasm. Don't make too much of this gesture. There's no nobility in it. It involves no sacrifice. There will be no wrench. It is simply the logical climax of a process set in motion before we met.'*

She too dug her heels in. *'I am determined to retain my own identity as far as essentials are concerned—the values that I believe in, the truths that light my path. As I have no wish for you to turn into a puppet for me to manipulate, I am quite prepared for you to reject any of my ideas which your conscience will not let you accept. So I, too, am unable to present you, by way of a dowry, with a list of sacrifices I shall be making. I shall not tamely espouse all Africa's causes. For the face of Africa, in this country, is not just the face of the immigrant worker, who endures the hardships of exile so that he can feed his family back home. Africa also assumes the loathsome face of those who sponge unashamedly on women in order to survive. I have heard so many heartrending stories, sobbed out by women with faces contorted with misery: women who have been the victims of promises deliberately broken; women who lost everything when their Black fiancés vanished into thin air with all their possessions. These women warn me to beware when I talk to you. But I tell myself that Love has not been eradicated from the whole earth because some affairs turn out so badly. All individuals are compelled to live by their own experience. I hope that mine will be successful. I am all Love and Determination.'*

And because she felt herself to be all Love and Determination, she would have liked to be involved in the day-to-day activities of the students' revolt, for their winds of militancy to fan the fire that consumed her.

But her father, strict as ever, played the part of the prudent lock-keeper, maintaining the sluice-gates closed to prevent the flood waters overflowing.

'No, my child. You're not going out just now. Not with all these riots! With all *that*'—his favourite expression for everything he disapproved of—'all this violence, you never know what can happen.'

In the hope that her father would relax his vigilance, Mireille participated only sporadically in the protests. But she felt as passion-ately involved as her student friends who were, for the most part, middle-class youngsters like herself, who belonged to the most militant wing of the demonstrators.

They abhorred the traditional nuclear family. They considered it an institution to be demolished, its contents revised, its power restricted, its limits redefined.

Monsieur de La Vallée was under the illusion that his authority and powers of persuasion had kept Mireille out of the inferno. When he came home from work he gave his version of the events—seen through government eyes—in the manner of radio and television reports.

But at night Mireille escaped to plunge into the inferno. Skirmishes offered an outlet for her fury. The violence of the storm revived it. And the thunder thus unleased gave a direction to her ardent yearnings for social upheaval. The inferno suited her choice of existence, and became an integral part of her unconventional love affair. During those turbulent times of unrestrained violence Mireille had two faces that she was adept at interchanging at will. The face of the placid girl living in the peaceful flat was less in character than the resolute countenance of the militant student.

What would her father say if he could see her, with her jeans rolled up above her knees, her hair blowing in the wind, her eyes flashing, shouting all the obscenities banned from the language of her home. Her mother would faint again if she knew that she was in the vanguard of the rioters, hurling any object to hand at shop-windows and passing cars.

Mireille wrote to her sweetheart describing the events that were
rocking the capital.

*'The objection to the segregation of male and female students in the same
University where the Minister for Youth had been heckled, was simply the
pretext for a latent conflict to break out.'*

Naturally Mireille was in full agreement with those who wanted
to abolish the established rules and regulations, while her father,
sickened by the events which he could not understand, grumbled,
'The youth of today! The youth of today! There's no limit to their
impertinence!' (His daughter noticed that he made no mention of
their courage.) 'Give them an inch and they'll take a mile. They
don't understand a thing. It's no use trying to talk to them. What
they need is a strong hand to bring them to heel. It's all the parents'
fault for not being firm enough and not assuming their
responsibilities! If I was the Minister, they'd be picking up the dead
bodies of their offspring! Then there'd be no more demonstrators,
no more barricades! No more protests!'

And Monsieur de La Vallée adjusted the braces brought into
service by his dutiful wife who worried about his loss of weight.
The state of Monsieur de La Vallée's nerves put a great strain on
his wife.

And Mireille wrote to her sweetheart, *'As for Mother, she accepts
everything that her husband says. She repeats to visitors whatever she can
remember of his diatribes against ''these lunatics'' (father's expression), without
giving them a chance to air their own opinions about what father calls ''this
tidal wave''.'*

Mireille concluded her letter: *'There is no longer any possibility of
doing things in the straightforward manner, as my father would like. Everything, hereabouts, is broken, twisted. He is thrown off balance by the challenges
to his concepts of honour, duty, obedience. But, for all his gesticulations, his
fulminations, as he continually strides up and down in the flat, the city was
dealt a staggering blow when it awoke on the morning of the 11th.*

*In the districts which the students had beseiged, the streets were strewn with
rubble. The unpleasant acrid fumes from the fires and tear gas still hung in
the air.*

*I was there, in the midst of the rioting. How can I describe to you the
heady excitement of finding this outlet, in the uproar and scuffles, for all my
hatred of convention? My happiest moment was when I landed a kick right
in a policeman's face!*

43

How I delighted in smashing up cars belonging to those sanctimonious gentlemen who preach fraternity and humanitarianism, and whose hearts are dry as dust! Oh, Ousmane! I had a hand in it all!'

The next day she wrote again: *'Negotiations have broken down. The workers won't accept the compromise agreements that the leaders of their trades unions have put their signatures to.*

Strikes are now general and the whole city stinks. The smell of dried fish that offends your nostrils in the evening when you get back to Grand-Dakar, must be nothing to the stench that pervades Paris.

Middle-class folk, deserted by their children, and left with only animals to lavish their affection on, are at a loss to know what to do with their time as they're kept indoors by the foul-smelling streets. And when these worthies do venture out, they have a job getting to a tree or a wall for their dogs to relieve themselves. Instead of disgusting heaps of dogs' mess that you tread all over the pavement if you're not careful, we have piles of refuse, tin cans, vegetable peelings, cotton wool, all sorts of garbage.

I can hear their prayers: 'Oh God, please bring back the dustmen! The barrow men! And the grocers! We're short of everything! Petrol! Money!

No more sign of that much decried abundance.

I continue to dig up paving-stones with my comrades. Our slogan: 'All prohibitions are prohibited' is still the order of the day.

We shall soon be together again.

Mireille.'

8

Carried away by the zeal and the illusions common to their age, Senegalese students, like their fellows all over the world, advocate the most extreme measures to change society. Reforms introduced by their respective governments are too half-hearted for them. They denounce these in vitriolic language, calling for violent upheavals. They dream of a just and fair society, based in some cases on imported ideologies and models, in others on an uncompromising nationalism.

Ousmane and his class-mates were not immune from the facile attraction of exaggerated language. *Keur Ali* (Ali's room in the university residence), one of their meeting places, often resounded with their passionate arguments, in which they dissected the revolutionary theories of Marx and Lenin, either demolishing or adopting them.

One Saturday evening Ousmane turned up there with a bundle of newspapers under his arm.

'For your information!'

Boly, the musician of the group, had his guitar with him as usual. As he sang the warsong celebrating the dauntless king Sundiata, the others nodded their heads or snapped their fingers to its rhythm.

'Sundiata Keîta!

Dômou Pinku dou dé!

Dômou Pinku dou daao.

Sundiata Keîta!'

(A son of the East does not die! A son of the East does not flee!)

This epic from their national history inflamed their imagination. Their voices paid homage to the African hero's courage.

'Dômou Pinku dou dé! Dômou Pinku dou daao!'

Once more Ousmane urged his friends to read the newspapers. But they remained under the spell of Sundiata, 'the son of the East who does not die, the son of the East who does not flee'.

Boly's fingers stopped plucking the strings of his instrument. 'If Sundiata returned to earth, would he recognise his descendants? Noble sentiments have forsaken the African soul. Look how many of our African leaders, who were in the vanguard of the movements for national liberation, are unrecognisable now that they have their

45

feet in the stirrups of power. Now they censure the very things they used to preach . . .'

This was another opportunity for venting their bitterness and disillusionment. They had been given their cue. One after another, or all speaking together, they let off steam. Their razor-sharp tongues tore the influential figures in the government to shreds, not omitting their luxuriously furnished villas along the corniche, nor their air-conditioned limousines purring along on petrol subsidised by the tax-payers.

Ali dwelt on 'dishonest officials who took advantage of their key positions to feather their own nests' and 'underqualified persons appointed to over-paid posts!'

He concluded seriously, 'As a result, you must expect to find them among the VIPs on public platforms, singing the praises of the progressive State, the humane Nation, the competent Power, the President, father of his people? The Head of an important government department admitted unashamedly, ''Do you expect me to chop off the branch that supports me?'' '

After Ali, the bearded student took up the attack. He caustically denounced speeches made by politicians: 'Hypocritical, high-sounding verbiage, strung together by unscrupulous technical advisers, and dotted with deceptive statistics to give the impression of seriousness and truth! And they all religiously refer to the President, at the beginning, middle and end of their bragging, as if he was God the Father . . . No-one dares cut the umbilical cord!'

These young people gave the impression that those in power were governing solely in the interests of the privileged, to the detriment of society as a whole. They bitterly refuted the arguments that were paraded before them, which alleged that they had no experience, no patriotism, no realism.

The one with the beard continued, raising his voice and gesticulating to retain their attention, in imitation of a minister holding forth: 'Doesn't the head of every family want his dependents to have the best possible home, good food, comfortable clothing? But when he compares what he would like them to have with what he earns, his family has to make do with a life-style commensurate with his means.'

Ousmane took up the argument on the same rhetorical note: 'A very good analogy! The head of a family who earns a modest living doesn't go squandering his money in nightclubs and casinos . . .'

Ali continued pompously, 'The head of a household who squanders his earnings deserves severe censure. It's a capital crime for a State to live above its means. It's a capital crime for a State to choose priorities that have no priority. A limited budget demands austerity and tightening one's belt.'

They often made ruthless comparisons between the trivial matters that were entrenched by hard and fast regulations and the urgent issues that were disregarded. They dwelt on the cruel problems of starvation, drought, sickness. They held forth animatedly on the question of social inequality and, even more passionately, on the yawning chasm that was swallowing up the country's wealth. They dreamed of turning the whole land into one vast building-site which would change everyone's lives.

And then they got on to Negritude! The student with the beard rose to his feet again to slam it mercilessly.

But on this Ousmane had the courage of his own convictions. 'I'm all for the general doctrine of Negritude. I'm for returning to your roots and keeping the way open.'

The others shouted him down. They picked holes in his suggestions for 'returning to one's roots' and 'keeping the way open'. Boly endorsed their sentiments by appropriate chords plucked from the strings of his guitar.

Ousmane concluded, amidst a clamour of opposition, 'Culture is universal. Culture is an instrument of development. How can you achieve this without self-knowledge which leads to self-respect, and without knowledge of and respect for others?'

No doubt they would have continued to be carried away by their own rhetoric if Ousmane had not suddenly stabbed his forehead with his finger, remembering a promise made to Yaye Khady that morning.

'I've promised to take my Mum to see Sembène Ousmane's film *The Money Order*. I've got to go. It's a long way to the Vog Cinema . . . I want her to have a chance of comparing the various neighbourhoods. What a world of difference between the "Vog", where the audience sits quietly watching the film, and our local "Al Akbar" with its hullabaloo and the smell of doughnuts!'

Boly snapped impatiently, 'You and your Mum! You're like a babe at the breast. D'you think the fact of taking her to a different cinema will turn her into a revolutionary? Anyway, your Mum's a spoilsport . . .'

Ousmane laughed. 'I'll tell Yaye Khady what you say about her. And she thinks you are so well brought up!'

Boly too took his leave and followed Ousmane out. His fingers danced over the strings of his guitar leaving the melody of Sundiata Keïta, 'The son of the East who does not die! The son of the East who does not flee', to linger on the air.

How Ousmane and his friends envied the students in France— those rebels in search of a cause—whose rallying-cry to revolt was simply 'Enough is enough!'

For their own part, they had genuinely serious issues to protest about. The matter of student accommodation was one of their most vital preoccupations: they had to fight to be allocated a poky room, comfortless—little better than a cupboard. Ali never tired of telling the story of how he obtained his room: 'The available accommodation in this university is ludicrous, compared to the number of students. I fought like mad to get digs here, it didn't help. But one telephone call from my cousin, who's principal private secretary to the Minister for Education and Culture, and I immediately got what I wanted.'

And they used to joke about the *clandos*, students who, like Boly, used lecture theatres and seminar rooms to doss down in every night. He defended his actions: 'What am I supposed to do? I live far away in the sand dunes, at Guédiawaye. It's so far that it's quite a surprise to find any sea there. The first person to visit that region was so struck by the sight of water there that he's supposed to have exclaimed, *"Guédié Waye!"* ' (The sea! Eh!)

His listeners roared with laughter. Still delicately caressing the strings of his guitar, Boly went on imperturbably, 'So how am I supposed to get home every day to my "seaside resort", especially when I have such a job to get here in the first place? There aren't enough buses and what there are, are crammed chock-a-block with daredevils who risk their lives to jump on. We must demand a car park to be organised and managed by the Students' Union. That would make an enormous difference to the transport of those of us who live on the outskirts of the city.'

Ali then drew attention to his protruding ribs . . . They forgot the question of transport to talk about food. They were very grateful to Yaye Khady who provided them with a meal of genuine Senegalese rice once a week. One of the students declared solemnly,

'If diarrhoea doesn't do me in, if the exams don't finish me off, then Yaye Khady, O Mother of Ousmane, I will show you what I can do for you!'

Other voices reinforced this promise, while Ousmane, embarrassed by the stream of praises, struggled to bring the discussion back to its proper footing.

'When you're cooking for large numbers, it's difficult to maintain the quality. But at least basic hygiene can be respected . . .'

But Boly did not let him finish. He made his bow, like an actor acknowledging applause: a few steps forward, an arm raised in greeting, a few steps back, another bow.

He said, quite seriously, 'I must be the first to weigh anchor today. I'm off to see my Mum in Guédiawaye. When shall we see changes in all this, my friends?'

Night was falling. Ousmane was the next to take his leave. He hurried back to Usine Niari-Talli. There was no sea in Grand-Dakar. But he much preferred the dust of his neighbourhood to the sea of Guédiawaye. Whereas he could get back home on his own two feet, Boly had to perform gymnastic feats to get onto a bus for Pikine.

But Boly had added as he left, 'I'm homesick for my mother. I haven't seen her for five days!'

Ousmane approved: the pleasure of seeing one's mother was worth all the jostling to get on a bus.

'Spears to slash social injustices!'

'Energy afoot to stamp out want!'

How could these students, who thought of themselves in these terms, not be tempted to extreme and violent action?

Most of them dropped out of university under the stress of hunger, leaving gaps in their already scattered ranks. Those who remained, pondered, fearing that this might be the death-knell of their futures.

Faint and scattered at first, the fires of contention suddenly flared up when the National Commission on Higher Education decided to cut students' grants. The flickering fires now developed into a dangerous blaze.

And so the city of Dakar also experienced its events of May 1968. The dense smoke of the eruption, that first rose ominously over the university campus, rapidly spread to darken the whole atmosphere. Trade unionists and unemployed, delinquents and layabouts made common cause in violent clashes with the forces of law and order.

There was a steady escalation of incidents: a cordon of police surrounded the campus! Shops, considered 'the strongholds of capitalism' were ransacked. Official cars were stoned. Trade union leaders arrested. Students detained by the police or sent home, after their rooms in the university residences had been searched.

When Ousmane's letters suddenly stopped Mireille was sick with anxiety. Then Ali wrote to explain her friend's unaccustomed silence:

'Ousmane was arrested during serious clashes on the Campus and is in detention at the Mangin Camp. Fortunately or unfortunately, I happened to be away in town for family reasons when the trouble broke out.

As Ousmane let me into the secret of your 'Post Box Yvette', I am taking the liberty of writing there to tell you what has happened, out of friendship for him.'

After twelve days' imprisonment Ousmane was able to resume his correspondence:

'I am sitting in front of your photograph and making a fresh start with you watching me. Your smile once more fills me with sweet contentment. I was let out of the Mangin Camp, with my comrades, barely an hour ago. An atmosphere of insecurity still reigns. The curfew still persists. Mother tells me that when she wanted to take one of her friends to the maternity hospital yesterday, she had to get permission from the local police station to leave the house.

For our part, we have no regrets. We had been bottled up beyond all reason and were right to erupt. But, for once, they put away their usual rhetoric and acted instead, mobilising the forces of order and endlessly employing the most diabolical means of repression. We suffered some casualties. But we are back on our feet and in good spirits, pleased with our victory, inasmuch as our struggle has made the authorities aware of our existence. They listened to violence, where they had previously ignored all peaceful means that had been employed in vain.

All educational institutions are still closed. It's to be hoped that this year will not have been wasted, which would make our period of waiting even longer. I hold you tightly in my arms.'

Law and order were gradually restored. After the revolt the university reopened. By the time the new term began the students had been given credit for their exams. The year had not been wasted.

Ousmane Gueye, intelligent as he was and motivated by his love for Mireille, his father's encouragement and his mother's loving attentions, made easy progress through his university courses. He never had any failures and so never experienced the discouragement that is the lot of even the most single-minded students who succumb to the stresses of the rigorous competition. He obtained his BA and then his Master's degree in philosophy. As an outstanding student he was again offered the opportunity of continuing his studies in France. 'I'll think about it,' was his reply.

For the moment his family needed him. The cost of living was rising. Even with his bursary, which eked out his father's exserviceman's pension, they could scarcely meet the cost of essentials.

His father was getting on in years. Ousmane knew that as a devout Muslim, who was constant in his prayers, he nourished a dream that seemed impossible for him to realise: to visit the holy places in Islam. Ousmane was anxious to pay for this journey.

And then, too, he wanted to get his family out of the depressing atmosphere of Grand-Dakar. He wanted to get away from polluted dust and air that reeked of stopped-up drains. He wanted his brothers and sisters to grow up in a decent house free from insidious draughts causing chronic bronchial infections. He could no longer make do with a corner enclosed with galvanised iron, when he wanted the luxury of a bath. He dreamed of a comfortable home for himself and his family.

He needed to start earning a living. So, with pride and emotion, he accepted a teaching post at his own former high school.

While Mireille continued to possess her soul in patience, Ousmane paid with his first month's salary for his father to make the pilgrimage to Mecca. And while Mireille continued to wait patiently, his application for an official subsidised house was being dealt with by one of his former fellow-students.

9

Mireille continued to wait patiently. She too had passed her BA and completed her MA in philosophy.

Like Ousmane, she too took a teaching post, in spite of her father's exhortations: 'You could go on to do your doctorate! You're not short of money. We can maintain you. What are you going to do with your miserable salary?'

But Mireille was firm. She hoped to save for her future home. Her parents might use her 'liaison' against her, but she would never have to reproach herself with using their money to set up house.

Her father had to give in. She went off to work looking pretty and apparently light-hearted. Her easy manner and forced gaiety hid the serious matters on her mind.

She continued to wait patiently. She indulged in casual affairs to obtain release from sexual desire. But she found these affairs unsatisfactory. These purely physical encounters were no remedy for her restlessness and inner emptiness. After every plunge into pure sensuality, Ousmane emerged in her mind supreme. The comparisons made her absent lover all the more desirable. The memory of their single act of love-making awoke a turmoil within her. Her whole being leaned for support upon her memories. They in turn filled her with an insatiable yearning for Ousmane.

So, every one of these escapades, every attempt at self-annihilation aroused an upsurge of remorse. Day in, day out, and night after night, she sought to reconstruct a new protective armour for her existence out of the fragments of her former happiness, until lassitude and exhaustion drove her once again into any open arms, to assuage her solitude and hunger. She grieved . . . She waited . . . While her parents thought that she had forgotten 'that object' the Black in the red shirt, she was still grieving.

Monsieur de La Vallée looked kindly on the interest that Pierre, the heir to an important industrial complex, seemed to be developing in his daughter. Monsieur de La Vallée dreamed aloud: 'Pierre is a good match, even if his name is a bit working-class. Mireille can keep her own surname. Pierre! The soul and the brains of his father's firm that his efficiency has given a new impetus!'

The Dubois, Pierre's parents, were wealthy. The de La Vallée family were invited to spend the winter vacation in their mountain chalet.

Pierre was not one of those dishevelled, long-haired youngsters in dirty jeans, with hands of doubtful cleanliness, who have nothing better to do than hang around the streets, lively or listless, dragging their lives like a burden. He was handsome, blue-eyed, always smartly but simply dressed; he had studied engineering and passed his final exams with distinction.

His upbringing had been based on principles dear to Monsieur de La Vallée.

'He's a good match,' Madame de La Vallée whispered, always in agreement with her husband.

As far as Mireille was concerned, her suitor was quite a pleasant young man. She appreciated his solid qualities without getting excited about him. She put up with his company, but she did not love him. Every day her heart yearned for the warmth, the sunlit landscapes of her Black friend's country. The link between them had been restored. They were united by their correspondence, filled with their love, their plans, their efforts to bring their future happiness closer.

She had skimped and saved, waiting till she came of age. And now, when everything was working out—the Gueyes had finally moved into a council house in the Gibraltar district of Dakar—she felt that Pierre was an intruder. She felt quite at ease in his company. With Ousmane, she had quivered.

The red roses that invaded the apartment every Saturday evening did not cause her to change her mind. To spare her parents' feelings, she did not tell them that she had refused Pierre's proposal.

But when they wanted to announce an official engagement she dug her heels in. That aquamarine ring, set in precious diamonds, would never sparkle on her finger.

Monsieur de La Vallée, supported by his spouse, stormed and raved. Pierre remained a good friend, always retaining an expression of desire and regret in the depths of his blue eyes.

10

One afternoon Djibril Gueye returned home from the mosque, after the Tisbar prayer and invited Ousmane to join him in his room. Yaye Khady was sitting on the bed, plaiting Safiétou's hair. Her skilful fingers separated off squares and rectangles on the little girl's head. She tied each little tuft with a piece of black thread that Safiétou passed to her from a skein that she was holding.

Ousmane sat down next to his mother, while Djibril settled himself in the only armchair, stretching out his game leg.

'Ousmane!' he explained, 'Ousmane, you are my pride and joy. You have fulfilled all my hopes. Ever since you have known your right hand from your left, your mother and I have had nothing to reproach you with. You have never wanted anything for yourself. You have sacrificed yourself for the family. In that you resemble me.

'I have trodden the holy places of Islam. I have seen Jeddah. I have prayed forty times at Medina, as it is recommended. I have heard at dawn the incomparable voice of Abdul Aziz, grandson of the prophet, calling the faithful to prayer. I have slept, intoxicated by my faith, in the Mosque of Medina. I have prostrated myself before the tomb of Mohamed Rassol. Thanks to you, Ousmane, I have followed in the footsteps of the prophet. My hand has touched the black stone of Kaaba. I have drunk deep of the holy water of Zem-Zem. I have hastened over the places called Safa-Marva which perpetuate the anxious journeying of Adjara, in search of water to bathe her new-born babe. Minam! Arafat! Moustalifa! Tamin! All the holy places of Islam. I have experienced it all. I have prayed everywhere. May God grant you everything, my son, *Al Ham dou li lah*! Thanks be to God! May God keep you, Amen! Amen!'

Yaye Khady and Safiétou echoed, 'Amen! Amen! Yarabi! Amen!'

Djibril Gueye cleared his throat. He looked his son full in the eyes.

'Forgive me for being long-winded, ''When the heart is full it overflows.'' My heart is filled with happiness. It needs to find relief. Let me tell you what is on my mind.

'Thanks to you, we are living here in this comfortable neighbourhood, surrounded by government officials. You could have come to live by yourself in this house that you obtained, leaving us squatting in our hovel like the young folk of your age who put their own comfort before their family. But you have always thought of your mother and me and our needs before looking after your own interests.

'But this house is far too big for the six of us. Your aunt Coumba pointed this out to me. This is what she said: ''Yaye Khady, your wife, is tired. She is fading away, for when youth marries age there is an exchange of blood to the benefit of age. So, Djibril, you are strong and fresh while your wife is withering, all the more so as she still has the responsibility of all the domestic chores, in spite of her age''.'

Yaye Khady interrupted angrily: 'Get to the point of what you want to say. If Coumba considers that I'm shrivelled up, I suppose she's suggesting that you take on a beautiful young wife! If Coumba thinks the house is too big for us, no doubt she wants to fill the empty space with a new wife who'll produce a baby every year, doesn't she?'

Djibril Gueye implored her: 'An end to your suppositions!'

Yaye Khady retorted with spirit, 'I'm not supposing anything. I know Coumba. She'll never stop pursuing me with her envy and hatred. Let her go and ask God to change my destiny!'

Djibril Gueye was shocked. 'Just listen a moment. ''Before you stop the mouth of the shepherd, first recognise the tune he is whistling.'' In spite of what Coumba may say, I don't feel so young any more. When a tree has borne fruit, it need have no regret at being cut down. Coumba's flattering theories about me have only one aim in view. It is not a question of finding me a new wife. Just reflect a moment. Am I such a wretch that I would instal a co-wife in my son's home? Coumba wants our son to marry her daughter Marième. Marième has been spending every Sunday with us since we moved here and she gives you a lot of help with the house-keeping. Coumba added, ''I count on you for making my wish come true. Ousmane is a good son. He is my son. I want him to be my real son-in-law. I'm not asking for any dowry, no sewing-machines, nothing but the sacred knot.'' '

Yaye Khady was so flabbergasted that she let go the tuft of hair she was holding. She was shocked by what she heard.

'What! She wants Ousmane to marry her daughter! After trying in vain to marry you off, you, her big brother, she's starting on your son. She's sick, I think, with her mania for marrying people off. Don't believe a word of this business of a "sacred knot". When a mother wants to get rid of a daughter she's all honey. "No dowry, no sewing-machine, just a blessing on their union". And once she's got what she wants, she shamelessly demands everything that's due to her. If she's not satisfied, at the first little disagreement she brings out her trump card: "Don't pick on my daughter. She doesn't owe you anything". And the daughter, too, at the slightest reproach gets on her high horse: "You married me without forking out a penny and you want to push me around into the bargain." So, Djibril, don't take any notice of Coumba's pretended favours. What I'm interested in is what you answered her. I know you've got a weakness as far as Coumba's concerned. What did you say to her?'

Djibril Gueye declared, 'I told her, "The billy-goat chooses its own mate." '

'Well answered,' Yaye Khady rejoined and, turning towards Ousmane, she went on, 'I may add that this Marième isn't very enticing. Ousmane, do you care for this girl who's as lanky as a palm-tree and uglier than a hyena? And she pokes her head in and out like a tortoise!'

Yaye Khady laughed, holding her belly and making the gestures to fit her description.

Djibril Gueye lost his patience and jabbed his stick at Ousmane, begging him to come to his assistance. 'Fortunately Ousmane knows Marième and is quite capable of making up his own mind. You exaggerate in shouldering on to the girl your quarrels with Coumba. Ousmane, what do you say to your aunt's proposal?'

Ousmane was caught unawares and realising from the way the question was put, what his father secretly desired, he made an excuse not to give an answer straightaway.

'I'm taken by surprise,' he said, 'and will have to have time to think about it.'

Djibril Gueye concluded, 'I prefer your circumspection to the way your mother lets her feelings carry her away. Always impulsive, is your mother!'

And to cut short any further discussion he asked his wife to bring him his grey caftan. 'The one Ousmane gave me, at the Korité feast.'

This was his way of keeping her away from his son. He was afraid she would try to influence him with her powerful convictions.

As Yaye Khady went over to the cupboard she had the last word.

'If Ousmane were to be told about all the mothers who are discreetly putting in a word for their marriageable daughters, we'd have no time here for any other matters. All my friends and acquaintances want him for a son-in-law. There's Ouleymatou's mother and Rabi's and Nafi's and Bineta's. My son is a man. You rightly said yourself that you don't let the females sniff out the billy-goat. Ousmane, and Ousmane alone, has the responsibility of choosing his own wife.'

To silence her, Djibril brought up a subject which embarrassed Yaye Khady.

'Don't forget that your father chose me to be your husband. It's current practice for parents to choose good husbands for their daughters. I didn't know you. But you weren't forced to marry me!'

'What do you know about it?' retorted Yaye Khady. 'Twenty years' difference in our ages and you boasting away instead of thanking God and my father for having given you such a good life!'

She burst out laughing.

'You were forced?' joked her husband. 'How could anyone force you, when you're as obstinate as a mule?'

'Certainly I was forced,' Yaye Khady retorted, standing arms akimbo. 'I was forced to marry you!'

The lack of conviction in her voice completely restored Djibril's good humour. Safiétou, who had no part in this exchange, took advantage of the respite granted her head to stretch her legs. She danced about in front of the long mirror, very proud of her new hair-do.

Ousmane had disappeared long ago.

11

Ousmane sat down at his worktable. After the second photograph of the 'film star' had appeared on the table, these had eventually proliferated to fill the pages of a whole album. The colour photographs looked like picture postcards.

'Wherever do you get all these pictures of a film star?' Yaye Khady asked him curiously.

'I buy them,' Ousmane lied.

From then on, Yaye Khady accepted that this was a collector's craze. Neither she nor Djibril Gueye had any suspicions, even when Ousmane handed them gifts 'from a white girl who used to be a fellow-student and who had gone back to France'.

Djibril had remarked, 'The one who writes all the time? The whitefolk like to write.'

He had received a fine pocket-watch which told him when it was time to be at the mosque. Yaye Khady's necklace had been much admired by her neighbours who asked her where she had got it.

'It's a present!' she replied curtly, refusing to be drawn. She knew that feminine vanity will stop at nothing in its search for novelty and she didn't want to see every bosom adorned with a similar necklace to hers at the next baptism.

It never occurred to Ousmane's parents that this generous friend from far away could be the same person who was present under their roof in the form of her photographs.

Ousmane's defensive strategy had not succumbed to time or to curiosity. With Mireille in France, nobody suspected his secret. He did not refuse to indulge in the pleasures that his age demanded, but these affairs were without consequence, and Yaye Khady did not urge him to marry, accepting his short-lived flirtations with girls in the neighbourhood, where he had a reputation for fickleness.

He began to correct his pupils' exercises with care. Aunt Coumba's proposal did not worry him. He smiled with amusement at the thought of Marième's portrait, as drawn by his mother.

He had to agree, 'That Marième is a real fright! She does look like a hyena!'

His parents' conflicting views about the girl would be his best argument if ever Djibril Gueye insisted on a decision.

His father had the sensitivity to guess at his refusal.

The fact that Coumba disappeared from the scene in a fit of sulks and that Marième was not in evidence on the following Sundays, proved to Ousmane that his father had intervened.

His gratitude took the form of a new walking-stick.

Dinner-time! The Gueye family was gathered on the ground floor of their new home. Yaye Khady was serving *M'Boum*, her husband's favourite dish, a couscous with cabbage leaves and ground-nut sauce.

Hands dipped into the common dish. From time to time Yaye Khady added another ladleful of sauce to the couscous.

The flavour of the *M'Boum*, cooked to perfection by Yaye Khady, loosened their tongues. Ousmane took advantage of the general good humour to announce his desire to travel.

'I'd like to visit Paris. I've applied this morning for an exit permit and a passport.'

Djibril Gueye seized this opportunity to reminisce once more about the country of 'his war' and all that he had got to know of it before his fall from the jeep which had dragged him along, breaking his leg.

Yaye Khady bantered, 'You must make an effort to see your film star in the flesh. They say these actresses have got no manners. Your Mireille (Ousmane had told her her name) is certainly a beauty. So she must be more stuck-up than all the others. When you have to rely on your looks to earn your living it makes you very hard.'

Babacar begged him, 'Won't you take me with you, brother? If I pass my School Certificate, will you take me with you for a holiday?'

Ousmane was more concerned to listen to the advice that Djibril Gueye had to give him over practical matters.

'It will be summer; nevertheless there are frequently treacherous showers and biting cold. Beware of the changeable weather. Your visit can be instructive if you use your eyes. You must observe and substantiate everything. You will make up your own mind, while comparing things with what you have read in your books.'

Yaye Khady warned him: 'I've heard that white women are on the look out for black men. Be on your guard. Don't bring us back one of them.'

Ousmane got up from the table in embarrassment and used the excuse that he had lessons to prepare so that he could be left alone.

He had no scruples about hiding from his family the real reason for his journey. His parents had agreed that 'The billy-goat chooses its own mate'. And Yaye Khady had added, 'Let the choice of a wife be his own affair.'

By hiding the real aim of his journey he put off the eventual moment of truth.

'What's the point of starting a fight before we need to?' he thought. 'We shall see . . .'

The school holidays were upon them. Examinations were forgotten and nervous tension lessened.

Ousmane found himself humming to himself, 'I'm going to get married! I'm going to get married!'

He was indeed going to get married, and this prospect filled him with a delightful sensation of lightheartedness that showed itself in an unusual extravagance of words and gestures.

He was going to get married! At last the dream he had nourished for so long was about to come true! Several months previously, Ousmane had sent the necessary documents to a distant cousin who lived in France, so that he could make the preliminary arrangements.

Yaye Khady found him transformed. 'So, here's another who's going to talk our heads off about Paris when he comes back! If Ousmane already looks so happy before he leaves, I wonder what state he'll come back in, when he's seen everything!'

And Yaye Khady felt a certain pride.

Ousmane feverishly prepared for his departure. He went shopping. Articles of Senegalese craftware filled his suitcase.

What should he give his fiancée as a wedding present, as proof of his love? He decided on a bracelet made of the most delicate gold filigree work in which Senegalese jewellers excel. He also took with him, at Mireille's suggestion, although it went against the grain with him, two wedding rings, as symbols of the state that he was about to enter.

A Boeing took off with three hours' delay, carrying him towards Mireille.

Part Two

Part Two

1

Roissy-Charles de Gaulle Airport! Already the climate and the technological marvels that surrounded him made Ousmane aware of the difference between the two worlds linked by the plane.

Before he could be on his way to the city, he was subjected to the close scrutiny of police and immigration officers, health inspectors and the meticulous attentions of the customs officials. But, after this trial of patience, there was the reward of Mireille, radiant with joy at their reunion, her milky skin and golden hair set off by the low-cut neckline of her blue dress, a touch of rouge on her lips and, in her excited eyes, that blue-green reflection of the sea!

Lamine was there, keeping discreetly in the background, seeing to Ousmane's luggage. Hands, which had been separated by time and distance, were clasped once more. The same intense emotion as in former times. The same affection coloured by intonation of their voices. Ousmane's ears were frozen by the cold air, but happiness coursed warm in his veins. Mireille gazed at her friend. She had left an adolescent. She discovered a man. But despite their greater maturity, his features had not lost their refinement. His open face still radiated the same charm and Mireille was not disillusioned. She had no regrets for the long period that she had borne the burden of her engagement, all alone, in this vast city.

Ousmane was entranced. His fairy princess was more bewitching than ever, here in her own environment.

The civil marriage ceremony was followed by a blessing in the mosque at Jussieu. The priest who officiated confirmed Mireille's conversion to Islam.

They had paved the way for every step which they were taking. They had nourished with dreams their long and patient wait for the moments which were now reality.

After a series of postcards which marked the stages of Ousmane's long journey, there arrived a letter from France which Babacar opened. The length of the letter was striking. Why did Ousmane feel the need to write so much when he'd only been in France a few days? Djibril Gueye's curiosity was all the greater since Babacar, who rarely lacked for words when confronted with this type of exercise, did not translate a single line.

'Well, go on, speak!' the father demanded, exasperated by Babacar's silence.

'My brother's French is too difficult for me,' Babacar replied. 'Give the letter to Monsieur Ndoye to translate.' And he took to his heels. With great foreboding, Djibril Gueye requested the schoolteacher's assistance: 'A letter from Ousmane. I'm looking for someone to read it for me.'

'With pleasure!' smiled the schoolteacher.

This is what Ousmane had written:

'Dear Father,

I am writing to you before communicating with my mother. You are the man who spent some time in a dahra, a man who lived through "his war", a man who life has not spared. So you are more armed against suffering than Yaye Khady. So it is right that you should be the first to be subjected to the shock of the news that I have to announce. I have got married here to my "film star".

She is the friend who gave you the watch by which you time your daily prayers. She was my fiancée. If you can recall the moment when you first saw her photograph on my worktable in Grand-Dakar, you will easily be able to judge the distance we have travelled together and appreciate that the rightful goal of such a journey should be holy wedlock.

If I have made a success of my life, if I am, as you say, your pride and joy, if I have fulfilled all your wishes, if you have left the dust of Usine Niari Talli behind you, if you can contemplate serenely the months and years stretching out before you, it is all thanks to her. It is difficult for a man to undertake anything alone. "Nothing can be done without a particle of love", one of my earliest schoolmasters often used to say. Mireille—I told Yaye Khady the truth as far as her first name is concerned—Mireille has helped me, by her unflagging moral support, to realise my potential.

She was always before me, like a flaming torch, lighting up my path.

She is not one of those common women, on the lookout for the main chance, who use black men to get themselves out of deep water. Mireille comes from a noble family that goes far back in time. Her grandparents still live in their ancestral château. Her father was a diplomat in Dakar, where we first got to know each other. Like me, she teaches philosophy. I have told her about my family. I have hidden none of our past difficulties from her. She loves me for myself and has renounced her own religion to become my wife. The mosque here has blessed our union.

64

You have the delicate task of informing mother. When you do so, lay stress on the fact that she is not "losing me". When you do so, think of the destiny of every creature that is in the hands of Allah, the All-Powerful.

Nothing can alter the deep feeling that I have for you.

We shall be seeing you soon.

Ousmane. '

Monsieur Ndoye had translated the last word. Djibril found the strength to get to his feet and thank him. He understood now why Babacar had run away, frightened of his anger.

Throughout the day, Djibril Gueye and Babacar kept their secret to themselves. But when evening came, instead of joining in the prayers chanted by the faithful as they sit in a ring round a white flag in the mosque, Djibril returned home.

'Back so soon from the mosque!' Yaye Khady opened her eyes wide in curiosity. 'Are you ill?'

He shook his head sadly.

'What then? An accident? A death in the family?'

He shook his head even more sadly and painfully climbed the stairs which led to the sleeping-quarters.

Yaye Khady followed him, begging for enlightenment. 'Tell me quickly! I can't breathe! Put me out of my misery! Speak! Is Ousmane dead?'

Djibril Gueye took his time settling himself in his armchair, stretching out and resting his game leg. Then he took the letter out of his pocket. Yaye Khady was in tears already, without knowing what she was weeping for.

'I was too happy. I've been too lucky. It couldn't last.'

In the face of so much misery, in the face of the sudden frailty of this woman who was normally of iron strength, Djibril made a superhuman effort to overcome his own distress and to fulfil his delicate mission.

'Ousmane has got married to Mireille, in France.'

And Yaye Khady, unable to believe her ears, repeated, 'Mireille! The Mireille in the photographs? Mireille? The film star?'

Djibril Gueye corrected her. 'Mireille is not a film star. She is a teacher. Your son begs your forgiveness.'

Yaye Khady drew herself up. 'Tears never helped anything!' She stopped her moaning. She dug out of her memory a thousand tiny clues which explained the present situation. The regular letters arriving from France ought to have put her on her guard. And the proliferating photographs too! And Ousmane's disdain for other women! She remembered the broken picture frame and Ousmane's anger when the photograph was left without any protection.

She had been stupid not to guess anything. 'You can't turn aside your fate! If I had only known! If I had only known!' She would have sought for the antidote to the spell by which this 'daughter of the devil' had bewitched her son.

Djibril Gueye, meanwhile, was carrying on a monologue consistent with his fatalism and his piety: 'Since this woman has embraced Islam, we must simply accept her into the bosom of our family. Ousmane Gueye owes us nothing more. The direction of his life is now his own responsibility. In the framework of Morality, he has the right to do what he pleases with his own life.'

Yaye Khady reacted indignantly. 'A *Toubab* can't be a proper daughter-in-law. She'll only have eyes for her man. We'll mean nothing to her. And I who dreamt of a daughter-in-law who'd live here and relieve me of the domestic work by taking over the management of the house, and now I'm faced with a woman who's going to take my son away from me. I shall die on my feet, in the kitchen.'

Djibril Gueye retorted quietly, 'If you had helped Coumba, Marième would have stayed with us.'

Yaye Khady stood her ground. 'I prefer to face this stranger than to have to face your sister Coumba. I don't regret my attitude. I may have to stay in the kitchen, but I remain queen in my own home. If Marième had come here, I'd be sharing my house with Coumba. You know perfectly well that Coumba would have taken over the housekeeping.'

Djibril Gueye lost his temper: 'You don't prefer the stranger! You can't love what you don't know!' Then, regaining his equanimity, he added, 'Let us welcome this marriage as the "evil" that is necessary for our survival. We have been the source of envy and hostility ever since our son made such a success of his life.'

He picked up his rosary. As he slowly fingered the big black beads he resumed, with growing serenity, 'Yaye Khady, let us say nothing of our sorrow. At this moment, while we are complaining of our lot, there are souls which God is carrying away. Between death and our suffering there is a deep abyss. Let us give thanks to God for having dealt us only those blows which we can bear. It is not chance that unites a man and a woman in marriage. Marriage is the result of divine intervention.'

Yaye Khady controlled her resentment. But she rejected the idea that this white woman was a necessary 'evil'. She left hurriedly, leaving Djibril Gueye to his prayer beads.

She quietly opened the door of her absent son's bedroom. She took the album out of the drawer where he kept it and turned the pages: they were filled with photographs of all sizes. Mireille was radiantly beautiful in every pose, sitting or standing, with wind-swept or elegantly coiffured hair, wearing a dress or trousers.

To Yaye Khady came the sudden realisation that this was the beauty of a Jinnee, an invisible spirit as capable of performing deeds of evil as of good, which had escaped from its own world. The spell that had bewitched and seduced her son was beginning to work on her. She closed the album so as not to succumb 'to the she-devil's magic'. But she was pursued by the wide-open, laughing blue eyes. The laughter in the eyes seemed to mock her.

'One is powerless against love.'

Suddenly Yaye Khady thought anxiously, 'Anyone who opposes love is like a person trying to dry up the sea. I have work to do . . .'

2

Yaye Khady tossed and turned in her bed. Night after night, ever since she had heard that 'her Oussou was married to that white woman', sleep had eluded her. She let out deep despairing sighs.

During the day, to prevent herself from thinking, she wore out her body with housework. At night, in spite of her exhaustion, she lay awake, gasping for breath.

She was overcome by a mysterious torpor, hampering her activities. The spoon in her hand had difficulty in stirring the rice in the cooking-pot. When she was alone in the house, the children out with their playmates and Djibril Gueye at the mosque, she would lie prostrate for hours on end, resting her heavy head in her hands. Ousmane had 'put obstacles in the smooth path of her life'.

'Oussou! The husband of a white woman!' 'An event of such great significance!' Her amazement never left her and she never ceased bewailing her lot. As a mother concerned for the welfare of her children she frequently had had occasion to consult charlatans, none of whom had ever foretold this behaviour on the part of her son. Someone was playing a bad joke on them. But the days went by and no new letter came to give it the lie.

'Oussou! The husband of a white woman! There are troubles which one whispers to a friend. There are sorrows which it is easy to share. To open one's heart often brings solace.' But what about her own feelings? What she, Yaye Khady, felt? Her soul was bereft of hope. Was it possible to live without longings?

Her heart hardened. Was it possible to live without love?

She was filled with bitterness. Was it possible to live on melancholy?

Her thoughts sadly ebbed and flowed through her head. The whole town would soon be informed, starting with her own neighbourhood where the schoolmaster who had translated the letter lived. This teacher would start the rumour on its way by breathing the news in his wife's ear, between their four walls, under the seal of secrecy. And still under the seal of secrecy, naturally, her misfortune would be peddled from one ear to another, made the occasion for encounters. Women friends, 'who only had her welfare at heart', would surround her to enquire whether 'there was any truth in the matter' and if so to assure her that they shared her sorrow. The 'matter' would be blown up, distorted, dissected, so that it could be spread more easily and nourish hatred and envy. It would be part of every ceremony. It would slip between two steps of a dance. It would accompany the choice of fish and vegetables at the market, squat round the public water-taps, beguile a couple of women travelling by bus. And she, Yaye Khady, she who had been the soul of dignity and honour since her earliest childhood, she who had lived in perfect harmony with her conscience, would, all because of her son, become food for all these tongues well versed in slander.

Thousands of invisible needles tore at her flesh. She grew thinner by the day. Every time she tied the ends of her pagne, she realised how much weight she was losing. How was it possible not to lose weight? The lump in her throat made her choke on solid food and for some time now she had been living on milk and broth.

Were it not for fear of Djibril Gueye's anger, she would have spent all day in bed. For his part, his faith made him accept the will of God without a murmur. For all her attempts to enumerate the pleasures that Ousmane had caused them, her torments never diminished. They sapped the strength from the hand that was scaling the fish. They froze her smile in a grimace when she made an effort to be light-hearted.

She mulled over in her mind how the children of her acquaintances had turned out, in an attempt to persuade herself that misfortune 'delivered its packets' at every door, rich or poor, humble or honoured.

Ousseynou Ngom, Ousmane's 'hut-brother', had dropped out of French school, unable to pass the exams. He was reduced to working as a shop-assistant, selling dress materials for a Lebanese.

Seydou Niang, another of her son's hut-brothers, was a disgrace to his family, spending his time loafing about the streets, good for nothing but picking pockets.

In their new neighbourhood the couple opposite had a son, a very queer youngster! This fifteen-year-old obstinately refused the company and games of boys of his own age and sought the company and games of little girls! A funny sort of boy this was, who modelled his bearing, drawling speech and activities on those of girls!

When his father came upon him, gossiping away with the old women, or cooking up dishes in the gutter, he went wild with rage and took a whip to him. But to no avail.

It was to no avail that his mother shaved all his hair off to make him ugly. You could still mistake him for one of the little girls he played with. He rolled his eyes as he spoke. And it wasn't only his eyes that rolled. He wantonly wiggled his hips and stuck out his bottom as he walked. As soon as he was out of his mother's sight, he draped himself in a pagne and strutted about.

'Nothing short of a miracle will stop that youngster turning into a *gôr djiguène*, a pansy destined to spend his life at the feet of a courtesan, doing all her dirty work. His job would be to procure generous lovers to keep that type of pricey household going. His would be the job of settling the accounts for the meals. And some-times it might happen that the clients would fancy him rather than his mistress . . .'

Yaye Khady was sincerely sorry for the mother of this specimen.

She also recalled the tear-stained eyes of her friend Kiné, as she went to call the police to restrain her son Moussa who kept the whole neighbourhood awake for nights on end, with his violence and his ravings.

Moussa was a complete junkie! He had been sent to Mali to stay with an uncle who had emigrated and to learn a trade; when he came back to Bambara he was unrecognisable. He had gone out of his mind under the rival onslaughts of alcohol and drugs. Moussa! A real bad lot who was in trouble as soon as he opened his eyes.

Only madness could explain Moussa's behaviour. He would break open trunks, steal the contents which he would sell for next to nothing to satisfy a thirst that daily grew more insatiable! Anyone would find an excuse to gossip about Moussa.

She calmed down. 'There's no possible comparison between Moussa and Oussou. I give thanks to God!

'And yet Ousmane and Moussa came into the world by the same means; both were the fruits of love!' Neither Yaye Khady nor Kiné had been under any pressure to marry. They had both been in love with their man. They had become pregnant at approximately the same time. As their bellies swelled they had both marvelled at the new life that was beginning to move inside them, at the little lives kicking against their sides.

'Every pregnant woman is filled with immense hope and proud joy. She feels a sensual pleasure in the ripening of the fruit of the gift of her body. She patiently bears all the suffering necessary for the successful outcome of her pregnancy!' Kiné, who was the first to be delivered, informed her that the pain of childbirth was like no other pain.

'You will see,' Kiné had finally admitted with pride.

And Yaye Khady had not 'seen', but she had 'felt' as if her body was being torn apart. She had been told that the child would be born when she managed to squeeze water out of a fistful of sand. She had not squeezed sand as she was shown to the Mandel Maternity Ward.

As her loins were racked with the excruciating pain, as fire raged in her belly, beads of agony fell in drops from her brow.

The infant in her lap had been the joy of her life. She thought, 'Every mother brings her own hopes to her child's bedside. She dreams a wonderful destiny for her little one, as she suckles him, as she cradles him in her arms, as she cares for his physical needs, but more than anything, as she loves him.

'The dream may end in muddy roads. Then there is disappointment. But disappointment does not mean the end of the struggle. Rescue work is set afoot, armed with a heart full of love and the immense need for self-sacrifice. And when all human and superhuman resources are exhausted to no avail, then the mother is left sitting on the ruins of her hopes. A disillusioned mother? Day in, day out, a stone crushes her heart. She knows no more peace.'

Yaye Khady pondered. Compared with other mothers, was she so badly off? 'The blind, the one-armed, the paralysed, all the physically and mentally handicapped, all the dregs of society, had all been born in pain and blood, in hope and joy. And what had the mothers of these blind and crippled done that they should find only a wall of shadows at the end of their long journey, instead of the hoped-for joys of childbirth?'

Yaye Khady pondered. 'A boy who turns out badly is preferable to a daughter who goes astray. The latter's depravity soon brings about her ruin. Stripped of her dignity, deflected from her role as wife and mother, she is at the mercy of every unscrupulous villain who exploits her in a thousand diabolical ways. Involved in dirty deals and sordid rackets! And when she's a worn-out rag, she'll never get any reward for all the humiliations. And her downhill path must lead inevitably to the ultimate degradation: to drag out her existence in a prison cell, to lie dying in a shady hotel; stabbings in squalid cafés or violent death in the street.'

Sometimes, when Yaye Khady had been in the maternity hospital for the birth of one of her own children, she had witnessed a scene of hysterical grief when a child had been stillborn.

'Blind fate has a predilection for the tiniest infants to satisfy its craving to destroy.

'The old man of seventy remains for ever his mother's tiny infant. So what does the age matter when death brings life to a standstill for ever? When her child dies, every mother feels her loins crushed beneath the same juggernaut. The same fire burns in her bosom. Her heart is caught in the same merciless vice. She is bowed down by the same impotence in the face of destiny.'

Tears rose to Yaye Khady's eyes. She wept silently for all those mothers whose infants die before they have 'drunk one rain-drop', infants cut down while they are trying to catch a golden ray of sunshine in their tiny hands. 'Ah, yes, merciless fate often wrenches a grown-up child from a mother's embrace. Grown-up children can die before the eyes of their distracted mothers who age overnight. And these mothers are condemned to drag out their own purposeless existence.'

Yaye Khady wept. And her thoughts proceeded laboriously, strengthened and comforted by this journey through life's vicissitudes. 'All the same, how could Ousmane have forgotten my face bathed in perspiration? How could he forget my endless drudgery, forget our mutual love? Will this woman relegate me to the kitchen for ever, then?'

What a world of difference between a black daughter-in-law and a white one! A black woman knows and accepts the mother-in-law's rights. She enters the home with the intention of relieving the older woman. The daughter-in-law cocoons her husband's mother in a nest of respect and repose. Acting according to unspoken and undisputed principles, the mother-in-law gives her orders, supervises, makes her demands. She appropriates the greater part of her son's earnings. She is concerned with the running of his household and has her say in the upbringing of her grandchildren . . .

There are mothers-in-law who act like veritable rivals to their daughters-in-law. They suck the younger woman dry with their insatiable demands and if it comes to a showdown they always get the better of it, as a single tear from them is sufficient to have the hussy repudiated.

Yaye Khady did not ask of fate to set her up as her daughter-in-law's rival. All she desired was the rest that she considered her due.

As her own parents-in-law had died before her marriage, she had not experienced the underground warfare that is daily waged between mother and daughter-in-law. But Coumba, her scheming sister-in-law, was always trying to 'cut the grass from under her feet'. So she had no dreams of crushing anyone else's daughter.

Yaye Khady only asked of fate the rest that was her due. Like all mothers she had had her share of those terrible sleepless nights when she had to rely on her instinct to diagnose a child's teething or the high temperature that might precede a childish ailment, when its life could be at risk. She had consulted healers, bearing payment in boubous or pagnes, for want of cash. She had had her share of queuing for hours at the clinic, getting up at dawn to see the lady doctor early, before doing her marketing and her cooking.

She deserved to be relieved soon. Many women of her age had nothing more to worry about than how to live out their lives agreeably, surrounded by praise and flattery, waited on by their daughters-in-law. They could remain in their own rooms, with everything falling into their laps: the choicest morsels of every meal, the ironing done for them, the bed-linen changed every day. At their age, it is right that they should be at leisure. If they were bored, they could spend their time scandalmongering. And they could fill their leisure hours with organising family ceremonies. Some mothers-in-law devoted themselves to God and killed time in this world by assuring their welfare in the next: they could be seen at prayer every Friday at the Mosque, perfumed and draped in white, like a ship in full sail, with their prayer-beads in their hands.

'There is no doubt,' she declared, 'one of the high points of a woman's life is the choice of her daughter-in-law.'

Ousmane was introducing an anomaly. 'A white woman does not enrich a family. She impoverishes it by undermining its unity. She can't be integrated into the community. She keeps herself apart, dragging her husband after her. Has anyone ever seen a white woman pounding millet or fetching buckets of water? On the contrary, the white woman exploits others who have to do the jobs for her that she's not used to doing!'

And Yaye Khady shook her head.

'The white woman manipulates her husband like a puppet. Her husband remains her property. She alone controls her household and all the income is turned to her benefit alone. Nothing goes to her husband's family.'

Thus surveying life's vicissitudes as she tossed and turned in her bed, Yaye Khady tried to obtain some relief from her distress. Her pious husband relied on God's justice, His infallibility and His wisdom to stifle any rebellion. Her pious husband, never failing in his religious practices, was right. The goodness of Allah succoured those who prayed, and she did pray. And then, compared with other parents whose love for their children had been as great, who had worked as hard as they had, compared to other parents who were as deserving as them, or more so, she and Djibril had been favoured by destiny.

Ousmane had respected and helped them. He had introduced modern conveniences into their new home. They were bombarded by requests to use their telephone, so that now they kept it padlocked. Every day neighbours sent food to be kept in her refrigerator. Her electric iron came to the rescue of many a mother in the neighbourhood when there was a shortage of charcoal.

These ruminations brought back her fighting mood. 'No! I don't care how white she is, no woman is going to play havoc with everything I've built up.' She wasn't going to let this woman be foisted on her like this without a word of warning.

She would defy this she-devil, with the golden hair of a Jinnee. She wouldn't allow herself to be supplanted. 'I won't let myself be destroyed to leave the field clear for her.

'This stranger won't easily eat up the fruits of my labours!'

This white woman who 'came down from her own hill' to intrude into the black people's world would see what she would see . . .

Not for one moment did Yaye Khady spare a thought for the other mother who, for all that she was white, had also given birth, loved and hoped. Her daughter had assuredly disappointed her by taking an unknown path. That mother was waging a different battle from that of Yaye Khady. Her love could express the same forbearance in its desire to protect. She was racked with suffering too, like Yaye Khady; it hurt where the umbilical cord had been severed; she too awoke to grief-stricken dawns.

Yaye Khady cared little for the torment of that mother.

White people for her were 'abnormal', not subject to the same laws and the same servitudes as black people! . . .

3

Mireille's family received their letter some time before the Gueyes. She had particularly chosen to send it to her father's business address. This summer morning the vast office, where Monsieur de La Vallée was going through his files had a holiday air.

He had taken off his jacket because of the heat. He saw in his mail two letters bearing the same Paris postmark. One was in Mireille's handwriting. Mystified as to why Mireille, who had left on holiday a month ago, should be writing to him, he opened the letter.

This was what Mireille had to say:

'My dear parents,

When you receive this letter, posted just before my departure, I shall already be far away from you, starting my new life with my Senegalese family.

I am of age and responsible for my own actions. I have embraced the Islamic faith and married Ousmane Gueye, a teacher of philosophy, first in a civil ceremony and then in the Mosque in Paris.'

Monsieur de La Vallée re-read these few lines to assure himself he was not dreaming. He repeated incredulously, 'Mosque', 'Islamic faith', 'of age and responsible for my actions'. Each word became a pointed dagger, piercing his heart. He repeated, 'of age', 'responsible', 'Islamic faith', 'Mosque', 'Ousmane Gueye'.

He put the letter down on his blotter and, looking round in a reflex action to be sure there was no witness to his weakness, he slumped forward with his head on his arms. He who was so strong, who always had a ready retort, resorting to this attitude of defeat! In any case, what control had he now over Mireille, who was of age and a married woman? Mireille, inaccessible and free, was snapping her fingers in his face.

'His name is inscribed on the little snapshot that was the cause of your bringing me back to France. Our love has survived the test of time and distance.'

The dagger, as if weary of stabbing, now turned its cutting edge. He pressed both hands to his chest, where he felt the pain, where he seemed to feel the jangle of those crazy words. For frightening minutes he could not get his breath; he closed his eyes and waited. The asphyxiating weight of the words grew less. His breath came more easily.

He seized the letter again. His mind reeled and his torture began again as he read his child's diabolically wicked words:

'Ousmane Gueye came to Paris to marry me. I dissuaded him from meeting you, to protect him from the humiliation that you would have inflicted on him. In your book, one can fraternise with a black man, but you don't marry one.'

He repeated, 'Of course one can fraternise with a black man, but you don't marry one.'

He was haunted by the memory of the blacks he had formerly employed as domestic servants. 'Hideous half-wits, guffawing with laughter, the whites of their eyes staring out of their vacant faces!'

What about the ones he had had dealings with in the course of his diplomatic missions? 'Even more ridiculous with their affected manners and their panting to catch up with generations of civilisation! They're primitive people! They behave like primitives!' And to think that his daughter would land up in these crude hands. 'What a mess!'

He read the rest of the letter through without a pause:

'You have loved me in your own way and I know what I mean to you. I am overwhelmed at the enormity of your grief. But one cannot escape one's own fate. I cannot give up the man I love, simply because he is black.

'I am turning my back on a protected past to face the unknown. I am aware of this. I am giving up comfort for adventure. I know that too. I say to myself that happiness does not fall into one's lap. It must be deserved. It must be worked at.

'Please inform my grandparents.

'If you can forgive me, write to me at the address at the top of this letter. If not, I must say goodbye, but with my love. My eyes are filled with tears and Ousmane shares my emotion.

Mireille'

Mireille was asking for forgiveness. She dared to speak of 'affection', 'renunciation', 'humanitarian virtues'. But her father's anger hermetically sealed off his heart against reason and love. Truth, as Monsieur de La Vallée understood it, imprisoned in a rigid armour of outmoded reasoning, did not admit any opposition. It was untouched by new and enlightened attitudes; it was unaffected by the 'extravagant nonsense' of the letter.

Jean de La Vallée was stunned. Pinned to his chair, he struggled for breath, sweat breaking out on his temples. He clutched the letter tightly in both hands as if it were a bomb that would explode if it touched the floor. Jean de La Vallée could not accept 'betrayal'.

'What effrontery! How could she have so little regard for the name she bears?'

Mireille had done wisely in addressing her letter as she did, to a place that demanded self-control, which did not permit him to give free rein to his feelings, a place governed by sophisticated protocol, where it is not admissible to give way to unbridled passions.

He muttered, 'Oh, the shameless hussy! What impertinence! She had the impudence to address her letter here, so that I'd get it with my official correspondence!'

At last he placed the letter on the table and slipped on his jacket again.

He felt a sudden chill in his chest and limbs. He left the office. His chauffeur was astonished to see him hail a taxi and get in.

Madame de La Vallée was in the kitchen with her Spanish maid, busy making a paëlla, her husband's favourite dish.

Hearing a loud, impatient ringing, she rushed to open the front door, without even taking off her apron. At the sight of her husband she went back to her cooking, simply commenting, 'You're home early!' Then she added, 'A surprise, darling. Paëlla for lunch!' Then, sensitive to the slightest irritability on the part of her husband, she asked anxiously, 'Did you leave one of your files behind?'

Monsieur de La Vallée stormed at her, 'The paëlla can stay where it is. What do you think has happened? A scandal! Mireille has married her nigger. Here's her letter.'

Then, suddenly remembering the second envelope, he added, 'There are even two letters. I opened Mireille's, the other's still on my desk. From the husband, I suppose. Into the dustbin, that'll go! Into the dustbin! But read this first.'

Madame de La Vallée hesitated . . . She remembered as she took the letter, how her husband had singled her out among several girls at a dance. He had been the first man to hold her hand and talk to her of love. She had been brought up in a convent for girls of good family and had learnt, among other things, the principle of obedience.

Jean de La Vallée, who was of a domineering character, had doubtless noticed her trembling lips and fearful glance. His bullying instincts must have foreseen a docile victim in this shy girl who blushed all the time.

Mathilde de La Vallée hesitated . . . as memories came back. When she heard talk of the problems of women's liberation, she remained indifferent. In her life, only her husband counted. She pampered him, obeyed him and anticipated his slightest whim. Finally, she read the letter . . . As a mother, she could share her child's despair as she was driven to this drastic measure. Reading between the lines, she could appreciate her dreadful dilemma. She was heartsick at the thought of the wrench her daughter's decision must have caused her. She was moved by the sincerity of her cry from afar. She forgave her. She opened her arms to cradle her child. In the autumn of her life, her maternal instinct was reborn. Must she forgo the possibility of becoming a grandmother?

But Jean de La Vallée was planted in front of her, inflexible in the face of this attack on his honour, this assault on his dignity. He exclaimed loud and furiously, 'Snake-in-the-grass! Slut!', by which his wife understood that there could be no reconciliation. And then, out of habit—thirty years during which she had not had a thought of her own, no initiative, no rebellion, thirty years during which she had simply moved in the direction in which she was pushed, thirty years during which it had been her lot to agree and to applaud—then, out of habit rather than conviction, she sobbed, 'Snake-in-the-grass! Slut!' and fell into a faint.

On opening her eyes, her only feeling was one of total isolation. Her daughter had disappeared into the night. She was sure she would never see her again. She felt plunged into mourning. The only person she had left was her husband, this cold man whom she must wait on, satisfy, applaud, till her heart broke.

4

Dakar-Yoff airport was agog with the excitement of arrivals and departures. Passengers struggling to register their luggage or get through customs, arguments with porters all added to the impression of a fair-ground.

The announcement that the Paris flight was about to land, on time, caught Djibril Gueye by surprise, as he imagined that flight timetables were based on someone's whims and so had been prepared to wait indefinitely.

The first passengers appeared, to be embraced by their families.

Djibril caught sight of his son. Marriage and rest had done him good. His skin had acquired a 'chocolate' gloss and he had put on weight. They waved to each other. Djibril recognised Mireille. She looked like her photograph. She was dressed in white trousers.

Mireille recognised the man with the stick as Djibril Gueye. Ousmane took after him: the same features, the same broad shoulders. Djibril Gueye was sporting his white embroidered boubou in honour of the stranger. Yaye Khady had brought out all his war medals to dazzle Mireille.

Mireille embraced her father-in-law warmly. The long passages in Ousmane's letters devoted to his father had given her a high opinion of him.

Djibril returned her spontaneous expression of affection. Mireille felt that she was accepted. They made their way out of the airport. A porter had collected all their luggage which they loaded into a van. They took a taxi and the convoy set off for the suburb of Gibraltar.

Mireille recognised the motorway along which she used to drive with her parents to the Petite Côte. Its two narrow carriageways rolled along impassively between the same wastelands lined with stunted hedgerows. A few villages on the outskirts of the town. The taxi lurched on the uneven surface of the road. At the Colobane bus station, the driver hooted impatiently as he forced his way through the dense crowds. Then he turned off the main road.

Ousmane reminded her of the landmarks: 'The Family Allowances Office'. Then, a bit further on, 'The Girls' High School, where you'll probably get a job'. A few yards from the school, 'The

79

Independence Monument! You remember?'

When they were stopped at a crossing by a policeman, the van with the luggage caught up with the taxi.

The convoy struggled up the dirt road that runs in front of the police headquarters and arrived at Gibraltar. Ousmane presented his locality: 'Gibraltar was built by the Department for Subsidised Accommodation and took over the name of the slum area that was here before, notorious for its palm-wine shops, brawling prostitutes, frequent fires and general insecurity!'

Mireille alighted from the taxi and clung automatically on to her husband's arm. Yaye Khady's name had not been mentioned, but her shadow hovered ominously over the group.

Yaye Khady first caught sight of Mireille clinging to her son's arm.

Up to the last moment she had hoped to see an ordinary-looking woman approach, whom the photographer's art had unduly flattered. But her breath was taken away by the reality of Mireille's beauty. 'A Jinnee!' she thought, 'escaped from her own world!' Those blue-green eyes radiated a bewitching, seductive power.

Mireille let go of her husband's arm and came forward smiling to greet her mother-in-law. She kissed her with all the warmth that she felt. Yaye Khady's coldness was all the more shocking in view of Mireille's affectionate greeting. Neverthless they embraced and exchanged greetings in French or Wolof.

Mireille looked around anxiously, inquiring, 'And where is Babacar? And Soukeyna? and Safiétou?'

Ousmane translated Yaye Khady's reply. 'They are invited to Aunt Coumba's.'

Yaye Khady added slyly, 'Has your wife heard about your Aunt Coumba?'

This was her way of reminding her son about Marième . . . A way of letting her come between Ousmane and the 'she-devil'.

Ousmane, feeling Yaye Khady's hostility, tried to ease the tension.

'Of course my wife knows Aunt Coumba and Marième by name.' He added with a mischievous smile, 'And Ouleymatou, and plenty of others as well . . . but she's the woman I love and that I chose to marry.'

Yaye Khady was silenced. From that moment she knew she could only rely on herself to get rid of the usurper.

The language problem did not help the relationship between the two women. Ousmane Gueye insisted, 'Hurry up and learn Wolof, Mireille, to make things easier for yourself.'

But Wolof is not an easy language and, in spite of the hours she spent studying with the Wolof-French dictionary that her husband bought her, Mireille did not make much progress.

She made an effort to get used for the time being to the community life, which upset her. The meals were always served in a large aluminium dish from which everyone helped themselves. After every meal the tablecloth was folded up and pushed into a corner of doubtful cleanliness. The water which everyone used to wash their hands was dirty after the first person. That did not prevent the others from dipping their hands in and Mireille did not dare to be the exception.

Yaye Khady, out of spite or habit, prepared extremely hot, peppery dishes which were torture to Mireille. They made her nose run, prevented her from swallowing and for days on end she had to live on fruit.

And Yaye Khady used the most trivial excuses to enter the younger woman's bedroom, intruding on the privacy which she could find only in this one room.

'Djibril Gueye is more understanding,' Mireille observed. Ousmane stood up for his mother. 'She feels frustrated. You must forgive her. She feels she has lost me. That I now belong to you.'

Mireille had to live for several months in this locality where Yaye Khady showed her off to her women friends as an object of curiosity and did not hesitate to bring them to the house, like a visit to the zoo.

But apart from the hostility which her mother-in-law found surreptitious means of demonstrating, Mireille was fêted. The sacred rights of hospitality were respected on the surface. Soukeyna, her husband's eldest sister, did her washing for her and acted as her interpreter.

When she was finally offered a post by the Ministry of Education, which made her eligible for an official flat, she couldn't move fast enough out of Yaye Khady's home and escape from her continual and annoying surveillance.

5

The amount that Mireille had been able to save over the years allowed her to fix up the flat put at their disposal. Her innate feeling for beautiful objects and her taste for interior decoration brought a pleasing, personal note to their home.

She indulged herself on fitted carpets and wallpaper. She did not stint on the furnishing of her bedroom. In the sitting-room the dominant colour was orange. Thick rugs, comfortable armchairs, lampshades everywhere, original paintings which she had brought with her from France, all set up a life-style to which Ousmane was not accustomed.

In one room she installed a desk and her collection of books: rare and precious volumes which she had received as gifts and carefully preserved, sets of novels and books for her work.

Ousmane Gueye appreciated his environment. His bathroom sparkled. Toiletries filled the shelves. His electric razor hummed each morning. Thick bath-robes and bath-towels big enough to drape yourself in like a pagne, hung from the hooks. Mireille was houseproud. In her opinion, people's environments influenced their behaviour. And in order to 'hold on to' her man, she tidied up and moved around the furniture and knick-knacks to find the best way of setting them all off. Her enthusiasm amused Ousmane . . .

Ousmane Gueye appreciated his environment. But, however agreeable the environment, is it enough on its own to keep a man at home?

The period when Mireille had had to live with the Gueye family had been a trial which had left its after-effects on both sides. Ousmane considered that his wife was possessive, 'self-centred'. The word had slipped into his mind and now it haunted him . . . 'Self-centred'. Yes, 'self-centred', and he recalled their first quarrel at Gibraltar. A performance of religious songs was being organised in one of the local squares. It fell to Djibril Gueye to preside over the ceremony and to translate the Holy Writ, in which he was so well versed.

Well before nightfall the children had set out benches and chairs for participants. Tents had been erected to keep out the damp and to create a certain intimacy. That Saturday night the square was illuminated with the harsh white light of electric bulbs.

El Hadj Djibril Gueye in his pilgrim's attire—white turban and burnous—officiated, surrounded by his co-religionists. Their role was to transmit his words, to fill in the pauses by hymns sung to God, to His prophet, to all those who have laboured for the supremacy of Islam.

Djibril had acquired a reputation, which had spread beyond the confines of the city, for his mastery of the art of translating the verses of the Koran, making them accessible to the common people. He was invited everywhere, but his game leg prevented him from travelling. When the opportunity to hear him occurred, there was a rush of his admirers, adorned in their best, for this spiritual feast.

In a voice full of feeling, the devout Djibril Gueye eloquently traced the path to the soul's salvation. His discourse was studded with quotations in Arabic and secular illustrations.

Episodes from Islam's early, difficult struggles emerged from the recesses of his memory and he used them to breathe an air of piety into daily activities.

'Djibril Gueye! He was magnificent that night! What is a visit to the cinema compared to an evening devoted to God? Why did Mireille insist on trying to deprive me of my father's oratory? There's always another opportunity to see a film, but you can't make up for missing these prayers.'

His wife, thus reproved, went to bed sulking. The intense pleasure that Ousmane experienced was a reward for his persistence and filial devotion.

Djibril, the eloquent soldier of Islam, attracted an attentive congregation. He thundered in his denunciation of Evil, gesticulated as he harangued the crowd and led them towards God.

And the singers loudly sang out the choruses to the glory of God and His prophet Ndiol Makâ, 'the Giant of Mecca'. The congregation echoed the praises. They clapped their hands. They nodded their heads in time to the refrain,

'Ndégam Rossol la khèye né mess
Kham nguene ne fi ken doufi dess'

'If Rossol (the prophet Mohamed) has disappeared, be assured that no man is immortal.'

Paradise was mirrored in their souls. In celestial Eden, women of incomparable beauty and virtue would fortify men's courage and inspire wanton spirits to repentence. They dreamed of rivers of sweet milk flowing through green pastures.

But they also meditated on the riddle of death. Those who have departed remain silent on the secret which they have unravelled. The gaping pit into which the corpse is lowered, bound up in its white shroud, remains a daily reality.

'To remain in this pit, till the last judgement, with a tube linking one's nose to the fiery fumes of hell.' No-one was tempted by this prospect.

And to redeem one's evil actions, to purge one's soul of its impure contents, to prepare for the life hereafter while still here on earth, one gave alms with their manifold beneficial effects: to bring healing from sickness, to obtain material prosperity, improve one's situation, postpone the eventuality of death. Alms are the only investment that will bring returns beyond the grave.

So, money, pagnes, boubous, and sometimes a gold ornament offered with ostentation, are heaped up in front of these soldiers of God.

Dawn broke over the gathering and no-one had slept. But no-one regretted having attended.

Djibril Gueye congratulated Ousmane on his presence.

'If you had not come, my words in defence of Islam would have been in vain. People would have said, ''Let him sweep up the rubbish in front of his own house, before he speaks of that of his neighbour''. Your presence here signifies that you have remained firm in your Islamic faith, in spite of your white wife.'

After a pause he went on, 'See to it that your wife's conversion to Islam is not merely a matter of convenience. The true Muslim is the one who prays. Teach her some simple verses of the Koran. It will be easy for her, since she can read. You must write them out for her in her own language.'

The father was thus indicating to his son, in this discreet and indirect manner, that Yaye Khady was always checking on them and had informed him that 'The *Toubab* does not kneel down to pray'.

Ousmane, uncompromising, relentlessly pursued Mireille to see that she carried out her religious duties correctly. This conflict was the cause of the first rift in their relationship. Ousmane was conscious that the breach between them was growing deeper every day.

Yaye Khady was in the habit of dropping in on them whenever

Ousmane deprived her of his presence for one or two days. But her Sunday visit was a ritual. She would burst into their bedroom, finding them still in their night attire. Then came her invariable complaint, 'Ousmane, did you say your dawn prayer? Ousmane, a man has only one intestine*. If you imitate your insatiable white woman, your sole intestine will burst and I shall be the only loser.'

The embarrassed couple would get out of bed. Meanwhile Yaye Khady would take the opportunity of sizing everything up and making her comparisons.

'Everything is clean and cosy and rich here. If that's a sign of success, then my son has been successful.' He was well rewarded, her son was, for his attentiveness to her and Djibril.

She would pick her teeth and spit on the carpet, fully aware that her action would spark off a quarrel after she had gone.

As Mireille cleaned up angrily after her, she remarked, 'It's bad enough to be woken up, as if the last trumpet had sounded! But can't she use the ashtrays for her filthy toothpicks? You might tell her so, without upsetting her.'

Ousmane thundered, 'You want me to forbid Yaye Khady to pick her teeth here? To hell with your carpet!'

'You don't have to forbid anything. You just have to teach her how to behave.'

'In my country children don't teach their parents how to behave.'

Mireille had to give in. But after every one of her mother-in-law's Sunday visits, at a time when the maid was off duty, she had to clean up her carpet, strewn with the fragments of Yaye Khady's neverending toothpicks.

Then Ousmane's cronies were always dropping in, out of curiosity or genuine friendliness, and would stay on indefinitely, having nothing better to do. Dinner-time would come around, finding the uninvited guests still hanging around her sitting-room.

Mireille, waiting in the kitchen to serve, was getting to the end of her patience. Ousmane would come through, demanding more places to be laid and enough food to be provided for the unexpected guests.

In spite of Mireille's protests the contents of the fridge were depleted: fish, meat, fruit, yoghurts, everything disappeared.

*According to popular Senegalese belief, a woman has two kinds of intestine; the name of the second, translated literally, is 'the intestine for gestation'.

And the chit-chat never ceased, kept alive with anecdotes from their childhood, when they were naked little boys together, robbing their neighbours' fruit-trees. They laughed uproariously. They shouted at each other as if they were yards apart. Those who smoked ignored the ashtrays and scattered their cigarette-ends on the floor. Those who chewed colanuts sneaked the bits under the carpet.

Mireille watched them from the sidelines: intellectuals in collar and tie forgot their Western culture when in the company of uncouth fellows in caftans, their former primary-school mates, with their heavily accented French. When they spoke Wolof she could sometimes guess at the subject of their conversations, especially when they burst into howls of laughter. They were completely uninhibited by her presence. No subject was taboo! She felt that she was treated with less consideration than a black woman! The traditionalists in the group violently attacked mixed marriages: 'A woman's only a woman, tall or short, black or white. So why look for one outside your own world? Marriage is a thorny enough problem as it is. Why create more difficulties?'

They praised the courage of their friend Ousmane 'who had retained the reactions of a black man', 'who had not rejected them, his old friends', and who, what is more, 'wasn't letting himself be dictated to or assimilated'.

They energetically expressed their approval: 'A black man who marries a *Toubab*, and keeps up with his father, mother, family and friends, is something of a miracle, and that's no exaggeration.'

Each one of them felt the wife's hostility, from her sullen expression, her obstinate silence. But what did that matter? 'Ousmane is the master of the house!' 'Ousmane's is the voice that counts.'

They despised Mireille's sulks and resistance.

Knives and forks were pushed aside. They joked about the tiny plates which couldn't hold enough to satisfy a man's appetite. Table napkins were grey after they had used them. The basin in the bathroom was like a kitchen sink, stained with grease after they had washed their hands. Moreover, even if Ousmane's cronies admired Mireille's figure and looks, they still ragged him: 'You'll never get a glimpse at that titillating little *djité laye*, unless you deceive your wife.'

Ousmane protested, 'Why should I deceive her? I can easily marry a black woman. I'm a Muslim. And so's my wife.'

Their eyes sparkled with pleasure. Their faces lit up. They fought for the most comfortable places on the couch, where they could stretch out with their heads on a soft, well-stuffed cushion. They made no bones about hanging their clothes over doors and windows.

Ousmane adored these social evenings which were torture for his wife. She expressed her disapproval. 'You don't just invite yourself to people's homes, you wait to be invited.' But the flood of Ousmane's cronies increased, every Saturday evening, occupying every chair and footstool and overflowing onto the carpet. Invariably the meal was followed by Moorish tea and endless games of cards.

Mireille took refuge in her bedroom. Her tears did nothing to alter her husband's obstinate attitude. His defence was inevitably, 'When you marry a man, you also take on his life-style.'

Certain aspects of her husband's life-style were most distasteful to her. Their mutual understanding, which was already weakened, was still further undermined. There was no question of Ousmane giving up his group and their collective life. He didn't even find these occasions a nuisance. All she needed, according to him, was a little understanding and tolerance.

'If your complaints were about matters of life and death,' he protested, 'believe me, I'd listen to them. But my mother and her toothpicks, an extra thousand francs a week to entertain my friends who bring good humour and warmth in exchange . . . I don't understand you. They're married too, and their wives put up with their absence. Some wives think their husbands have got a mistress. But you've got me under your eyes the whole time. You know what we're up to. Come on, Mireille! Show a bit of good will!'

But Mireille had her own concept of family life. She had grown up, from earliest childhood, in a world where one did not ask of others more than they were prepared to give.

She grew tired of complaining, and Ousmane Gueye, thinking that she had adopted his principles, granted himself even greater liberties.

6

On the same landing of the block of flats where Mireille and Ousmane lived, there was a European couple of their age.

The husband could not pass Mireille without wincing. Genevieve, his wife, a French provincial girl, small, dark and plump, had neither the beauty nor the refinement nor the charm of Mireille. As soon as he was inside his own front door he would burst out, 'Can you imagine? That beautiful French flower in the hands of that lout! How can that nigger appreciate her, with that hair, those eyes, that aristocratic air? I could explode!'

Genevieve calmed him down. 'She's not your sister, nor any relative of yours. Everyone has to take responsibility for their own choice. Why should you torment yourself if she's happy in her present situation?'

'Her husband's never at home. He gets his own way in everything. She's always alone. I sometimes catch an expression of great sadness in her eyes. I've got the impression that things are not going well.'

'You've got the wrong impression. Why should she be unhappy? Her husband adores her. They were courting for ages. She told me their story, a long story of love and fidelity. Ousmane went to France to bring her back. You're making things up. And if you don't stop spying on her, I'll be the one to make a scene. You take more interest in her than in your own wife, I do declare!'

Guillaume was forced to eat his words. But he was haunted by 'Beauty and the Beast', as he nicknamed the mixed couple. It was not that he was in love with Mireille, but he was prejudiced against mixed marriages. Nevertheless he maintained good relationships with his black colleagues, male and female, whose hospitality and friendship he appreciated.

He and his wife had been invited by 'Beauty and the Beast' to a meal of fish and rice, cooked by Soukeyna. They laughed together over the howlers which peppered their pupils' exercises.

Ousmane Gueye was anxious to know from Guillaume how he found the local schoolboys. 'Is their level lower than the one you were used to?'

He was given an honest answer: 'They're neither more stupid

nor more intelligent. But they work harder here. At home it's become so important that the child shouldn't be "frustrated" or "got at" or whatever, that someone's forever thinking up something to make the pupils' lives easier and to bedevil the teacher, and so the kids get lazier and lazier. Till they don't make the slightest effort!'

Ousmane Gueye warned him, 'They're starting the same rubbish here too. Whereas I used to walk miles to get to school, I see my pupils arriving on bikes or motor-bikes. But they've left their exercise-books at home. Fathers are worried about the distance their kids have to travel, but not about whether they've done their homework.'

Sometimes Ousmane took the discussion a little deeper. 'We all belong to the generation of May 1968. Our motivation was different, but we had the same dream of revolutionising and reforming the world. Now that you're in the "old fogies' camp", what do you think of the attitude of the present-day students?'

Guillaume took up the challenge. He scratched his head, turned to his wife for support and replied in his sing-song Southern accent, 'When you're young, you sometimes behave irresponsibly. My mother often says, "Young people are still near to the angels, and so they think miracles are possible, and they want heaven on earth." So . . . at that age, they idealise everything. At that age too, it is easy to criticise. Nowadays I can see the necessity of everything that I used to jump all over: rules and regulations, discipline, strictness, hard work etc. Nothing can last without support. A building can't hold without foundations. A country without a sound government collapses. One can't satisfy every appetite at one and the same time. Every social class has its priorities and its demands. Political authority also has its priorities and its demands. Its activity is limited. It acts as a pilot, but it can't navigate if it is threatened with shipwreck.'

Genevieve confirmed his attitude. 'I'm being paid back for all the tricks I used to play on my teachers. A rowdy class can't get on. No matter how much effort you put into your teaching, you can't get any lasting results. Now that I'm in the hot seat, I look back with admiration at my former teachers' self-control. I appreciate their will-power in sticking to their job in the midst of all that organised pandemonium.'

Ousmane agreed. 'I share your opinion. I was one of the most militant of the May '68 students. I think we went too far. With the passage of time, we can view the situation dispassionately. We choose as our models those societies where we thought life was easier and better, because it was more organised. Those models now seem far from perfect. Liberty is often seen to be stifled, or measured out drop by drop, to see that everyone gets the same dose. People may dance, to be sure, but they must keep in step. No-one has the right to choose his own rhythm.'

Mireille added her ironic comment: 'The grass is always greener on the other side of the fence. There, it's all singing and dancing. But on my side, everything is dreary and bleak.'

Ousmane went on, 'When all's said and done, all governments are alike. It's six of one and half a dozen of the other.'

And, after a pause, he added thoughtfully, 'Those who can still say what they think out loud, as they can here in Senegal, without the risk of being locked up, can consider themselves lucky.'

Mireille showed Genevieve how to make 'Moorish tea' in a little metal teapot and served in small glasses. The pale yellow infusion, slightly sweetened and flavoured with mint, helps the digestion.

Genevieve and Guillaume, 'the two G's' as Ousmane and Mireille nicknamed them, thanked them for their hospitality and returned to their own flat.

Genevieve insisted that they must ask the Gueyes back. 'We must return their hospitality and their kindness.'

But Guillaume would not hear of having 'Beauty and the Beast' at his own table.

'I can stand them in their own home. But here, in my place, it's unthinkable.'

And he continued to take a fiendish delight in spying on them. His instinct told him, from the girl's tea-dimmed eyes, that things were going wrong with 'Beauty and the Beast'.

7

One day, as Mireille came home from shopping, she complained loudly, 'I'm not going to get a wink of sleep again tonight.'

'Why not?' asked Ousmane, puzzled. 'Aren't you well?'

'I'm perfectly well, thank heavens. But as I came back from the market I saw them setting up benches and tents on the square, the whole prelude to some nocturnal event.'

'Just stop up your ears. *I*, on the other hand, will have the pleasure of reliving the nights of my childhood.'

One more ground for friction! It was not that Mireille didn't appreciate African music. But the tomtoms drumming right through the night! It set her nerves on edge and her temples throbbing. And by depriving her of her much-needed sleep it caused her to lose her sense of proportion. And what with the prospect of the 'cronies' invading her sitting-room on top of the tomtoms thudding in her head and the next morning's visit from Yaye Khady, this was the last straw. 'We saw everything through the same eyes before we were married,' she stormed. 'But now we seem to be divided over everything.'

Ousmane looked at her. 'I live as it is right for me. I love the tomtom. You adore Mozart; you can listen to him all night. Just accept that I like the tomtoms. You can't understand. The tomtom is the black man's whole life bursting forth in sheaves of sound: the rhythms of the sowing season, the harvest time, rhythms of rain and baptisms and prayers; and sometimes even the rhythm of death. The tomtom marks the stages of our life. I can see myself as a child, in the boubou I wore for my circumcision: a wide rectangle of cotton sewn up at the sides, with a hole in the middle to go over my head. A pointed cap of the same material was tied under my chin. White amulets were hung round my neck to ward off sorcerers' evil eyes, and two cowrie shells on my forehead to protect me. There were ten of us little boys of the same age, dancing at night round the fire for which we had gathered wood during the day to light up the scene. The initiation songs filled the air, accompanied by the tomtoms . . . We underwent our apprenticeship of virility and courage. The tomtom compensated for all the cruelties that we had to endure, which made men of us . . .'

At this point in his reminiscences Ousmane turned round. He wanted his wife to share the emotions that his memories brought back. The song of the toad, *'ndoti ndoti samamou lin lin'*, rose to his lips from his innermost being. But Mireille had long ago disappeared into the kitchen.

So Mireille would never follow him. He bitterly surveyed the lack of understanding that separated them: an ocean. He must immerse himself in the heart of his own race, to live according to black values and the rhythmic beat of the tomtom. He was drawn by his past, by his nature, to assume with fervour his own cultural heritage:

Folktales? He could break open their shell to reveal their hidden kernel—the lessons in community living that their comic or dramatic episodes illustrated.

Proverbs? Their concise formula, carved out of ancestral wisdom, through meditation, observation and experience, went back to the very origins of life.

Legends? The expression of a creative imagination. Magnifying reality, they fortify a people by celebrating virtue. So many epics live on in memory to ensure the survival of history, thanks to legend!

How could he get his wife to share these truths, if she refused the most accessible of emotions, music?

African music! Now it bursts forth from the powerful voice of the female musician who covers her ears with her hands, now roaring in the throat of the inspired *diali*, faced with an attentive audience. Now its subtle notes arise from the stretched strings of the *kora*, that the practised fingers scarcely skim, now from the *gorong, tama sabar* or *ndeud*, now it soars aloft from the balafon, or tinkles with the swinging of little bells! . . . African music is universally appreciated. It cannot be dissociated from its natural accompaniment, the tomtom.

And Ousmane waxed indignant.

'The black race is not a race destined to go naked! Blacks have cut and fashioned prestigious apparel from their souls and hearts. The *griots* hand down our patents of nobility!'

Now he was almost shouting: 'The black does indeed know how to give, and to give of himself, even if his generosity has to drain the last drop of his blood or the last penny of his budget!

'*Kersa, soutoura, ngor*! Modesty, reticence, dignity and honour! These are the qualities that helped the slaves to survive those terrible crossings over raging seas, their legs shackled, exposed to the humiliation of the whips. These same qualities led to the cultural renaissance of the African continent and to the reunion of brothers long separated. Our qualities have helped in the spectacular revival that we are witnessing today.'

He concluded, 'Black scholars are demonstrating the close cultural and linguistic links between the Bantu and the Egyptians!'

His spouse had finally deigned to abandon her domestic activities, but remained unmoved by his flights of eloquence. And so the rift that separated them increased. No-one can be satisfied by feelings that are solely based on the appeal of the senses. Each of them lived encapsulated within themselves.

Ousmane was irritated by Mireille's meticulousness, her mania for organising, her insistence on clear-cut distinctions which led to endless classifying and reclassifying. They were still able to communicate in certain fields of conjecture, but Ousmane was racked by innumerable problems, difficult to formulate, which required urgent solutions.

He caught himself wishing, 'Oh, to find an echo to my own voice! To find a kindred soul, tormented by the same thirst! To find the partner, prepared to make the same fantastic journey through life, receptive even to the howl of the hyena, a shepherdess fascinated by the myriad stars in the sky!'

He had studied his wife's culture deeply: her rich past had achieved renown in every field; he understood and accepted this past.

So why did his wife not make the same effort to accommodate him? Her all-or-nothing attitudes upset him. Was it too much to expect of a wife that she have a little more understanding of the person who looks to her for support? Can a person be expected to change his mentality and habits and way of life overnight?

Mireille's lack of sympathy grew worse. She was inflexible, indignantly condemning behaviour which she qualified as 'lack of breeding', 'impertinence', 'lack of consideration' or 'vulgarity', according to the circumstances.

More arguments. Everlasting arguments! Ousmane Gueye had had an interminable attack of 'flu. Yaye Khady thought that her son's last days had come.

'The *thiat*. The evil eye! An illness that doesn't respond to injections and tablets must be the work of charlatans!'

93

And how many charlatans did she not consult! She ran backwards and forwards from her own home to her son's flat, bringing powders that must be left to smoulder in an incense-burner, stinking out the whole atmosphere, or some holy water—a dubious liquid which she sprinkled over Ousmane, staining the sheets and blankets, or an amulet which she hung round his neck or his waist, or on his arms or legs, according to prescription.

For Mireille, this daily invasion of her privacy was unheard of. Yaye Khady even had the effrontery to hang a horn on the door of her bedroom! And Djibril Gueye backed her up by settling into the flat every day at sunrise, to recite protective verses of the Koran.

Mireille put up with these violations of her home, for fear of making her husband's condition worse.

At last! Ousmane Gueye slowly got the better of his illness. The doctor, who had been consulted simultaneously with the charlatans, finally brought down his high temperature and the delirium ceased —both symptoms interpreted by Yaye Khady as due to the power of her sorcerers.

Ousmane's vomiting and lack of appetite had been attributed by Yaye Khady to stones with which sorcerers had filled his belly.

Yaye Khady stayed less and less in Gibraltar, even after her son was well enough to go back to work. She made herself responsible for overseeing her son's complete return to health. She came every day to admire her child's renewed strength. She came every day and bottles and potions continued to waltz through the flat.

Mireille, at the end of her patience, suggested that she should stay at home.

'Ousmane is better. I am quite capable of ensuring his convalescence by myself, feed him up and see that he doesn't overdo things.'

Yaye Khady retorted furiously, 'You think you can build up a man's strength with your bits of beefsteak, an apple and a yoghurt? Ousmane needs building up. He needs to train his stomach and intestines to digest food again with a dish of *foufou*. And an ox-foot soup to give him back his strength. I shall come every day to bring him what he must have. If you've no objection!'

Mireille was taken aback when the houseboy translated this speech. She decided that Ousmane must settle the argument.

But Ousmane was met by Yaye Khady in tears, who explained between her sobs and sniffs, 'Your wife has thrown me out. She told me never to set foot here again.'

Mireille countered, 'I have put up with all these disgusting smells. I have put up with this horn, hung on my bedroom door, and my soiled sheets. Now that you are better, I demand that my privacy be respected. Yaye Khady won't understand that this is not her home!'

To his wife's stupefaction, Ousmane sided with his mother and shouted, 'If you can't stand Yaye Khady's presence here, then you can get out . . .'

Mireille was speechless. She had difficulty in getting her breath. The blood surged to her head. She seemed to be suffocating; something was choking her, slowly, blacking out the outside world. She fainted.

Yaye Khady's cry of fright alerted the two G's. They carried Mireille into the bedroom. Guillaume slapped her cheeks, Genevieve bathed her forehead with eau de cologne.

Mireille came to as from a nightmare. Tears trickled down her cheeks. Ousmane Gueye stared at her without a single gesture of affection, to avoid vexing his mother. Yaye Khady fled. But once again, she had been the cause of something indefinable but essential deserting the couple's relationship.

30

The gynaecologist had confirmed that a new birth could be expected. As Mireille grew larger, with the new life quickening within her, she was moved to modify her attitudes. She clung to this miracle 'a life within a life', to restore the harmony of their home.

She made every sincere and affectionate effort to reduce the many differences that now separated her from Ousmane.

A brief respite! Then resumed hostilities . . .

Mireille excluded Ali and Boly, now both married, from the host of Ousmane's 'undesirable cronies'. Rosalie, Ali's wife, had been on the secretarial staff of the university administration during their student years. She was a Muslim, in spite of her Christian-sounding name.

Yaye Khady admired her and let it be known, 'Rosalie has no reason to envy Mireille!' She went into ecstasies over Rosalie's 'refinement' and 'adaptability', her respect for tradition and her willingness to give her in-laws their 'due'.

'You don't have to go to foreign parts to find a "good" wife. Black women can compete with white girls in every respect. Ali has made a good choice, and in his own world. Rosalie is a "real wife".'

And Rosalie, in her capacity as a 'real wife', initiated Mireille into the social conventions of Senegal. She explained to her a wife's relationship to her husband's family.

She advised her, 'Go and visit your parents-in-law alone, without your husband. They will appreciate the trouble you have taken and the fact that no-one is behind you, forcing you . . . From time to time send Djibril Gueye dishes that you have prepared specially for him. We have a saying, "The mouth that chews is always grateful to the hand that provides".

'Always have a coin ready, or better still, a banknote, to help your visitors on their way, especially if they are your in-laws . . .

'Don't forget to give your parents-in-law something new to wear at the Korité and Tabaski celebrations. Ousmane's brother and sisters also expect handsome presents . . .

'Don't shut yourself up in your room brooding when your husband is entertaining his friends. A cheerful welcome from you will be your trump card if outsiders try to break up your marriage. The good turns that pals can do are incalculable, compared with the damage they're responsible for. A pal is sacrosanct; he has certain recognised rights and his advice is always heeded.

'An inhospitable wife wraps her husband in a tissue of ridicule. Watch your step! Ousmane Gueye is proud!'

Rosalie considered the obstacles that could hamper Mireille's progress along the tortuous paths of this society.

'I can't insist too much on the need to give. Here, more than anywhere else, giving solves many problems.'

So Mireille wore herself out trying to follow her friend's instructions. But habit prevails. It can be traumatic to modify one's behaviour, to aspire to a completely different goal. 'If you leave your habits at the threshold of a house, they will run after you if you don't hurry back for them,' the saying goes. And Ousmane Gueye made no attempt to hide his contempt for his wife's efforts at adaptation.

So it was not long before Mireille forgot Rosalie's advice. She did not particularly relish the idea of having to distribute money every day. Ousmane's cronies lingered on in the sitting-room till she was forced to turn them out, saying, 'This isn't an old-clothes dump'.

The 'meals' that she prepared for Djibril Gueye on Saturday evenings caused Yaye Khady to laugh in her face.

'One chicken in a soup-tureen for your husband's father! What can you be thinking of? For the father-in-law one cooks at least five chickens.'

How could she invite her women friends to show off Mireille's generosity? Her friends would be flabbergasted at the sight of one miserable chicken swimming in a lake of sauce.

Mireille was angry. The extravagance which was expected of her was beyond her comprehension. Didn't she take her parents-in-law, at the end of every month, their allowance to cover their expenses? In her annoyance she gave up the Saturday meals.

Yaye Khady accused her, 'If you do nothing you understand nothing. Money that's earned is meant to be spent.' And knowing nothing of Mireille's own finances, she warned her angrily, 'You're sitting on my son's money. I'll find the means of dislodging you some day.'

Mireille flushed. She could not accept the demands of a society that was completely orientated towards outward appearances, in search of status, and in which her husband seemed remarkably at ease.

Mireille envied Lamine's wife, Pierrette. Lamine had been Ousmane's witness at their wedding. Pierrette's parents had given her marriage their blessing. What is more, they had organised a party when their daughter left for Africa.

Every year, Pierrette's mother would escape from the European winter to enjoy the African sunshine, making no bones about staying with Lamine.

Mireille envied Pierrette. Lamine had an open mind and was not tormented by ideological complexes. His negritude did not sit heavily on him. For him, it was neither a defect to be eradicated nor a value to be proved, but something to be accepted and lived with, without any obsession. None of his attitudes betrayed any sign of inner disquiet. Unlike Ousmane, he did not go about with one ear cocked for what 'his own people' had to say. He simplified his life by dissociating himself from African circles and adopting Western ways. He gaily turned his back on social conventions which had no real meaning for him. His family considered him 'a lost soul'.

'Has he ever been seen inside a mosque?'

'Has he ever been seen in traditional dress?'

These malicious comments did not worry him. He paid no attention to the slanderous allegations that wine and pork, 'anathemised by the Koran', had the place of honour on his table.

Lamine went happily on his way, with Pierrette at his side. He had named his youngest daughter Solange-Khadidiatou. But the memory of 'Khadidiatou' was buried and only 'Solange' survived. It irritated Ousmane to hear his niece answer only to the 'ridiculous' name of Solange.

Lamine did not involve his wife in his obligatory family visits, which were occasions for mutual sizing-up rather than socialising. Pierrette, for her part, had kept her in-laws away from her home, and her husband did not take this amiss.

'You're completely assimilated, old man,' grumbled Ousmane.

'You can't combine two different conceptions of life', Lamine argued. 'If you're to be honest, you've got to make a choice. *You* want happiness without making any sacrifices. *You* won't make any concessions, while demanding concessions from others. Married life is based on tolerance and a human approach.'

Lamine went on seriously, 'Difficulties arise from dissimilarities in personality, from decisions that have to be made, from the different interpretations that each partner gives to the word "happiness".'

Mireille was undergoing two difficult apprenticeships: that of married life and that of a black man's wife in Africa. Over and above the endless round of normal conflicts, inherent in the life of any couple, she suffered from other attacks. She felt as though they wanted to bury her alive and resurrect her as another woman who would have nothing in common with her except her physical appearance. But she resisted. She made it quite clear that she saw things different from the people around her. She was shaken in her most firm and innermost convictions and every day eroded a little more of the courage with which she had armed herself when she left her own country and turned herself into a rebel.

Ousmane did not change. His habits, deeply rooted in his childhood, remained immovable. He preferred a spoon to a fork. He could sit down to eat without washing his hands. When he left the bathroom, the floor was flooded, as he didn't bother to control the water from the shower. The bath-towel, well in evidence, did not prevent him drying himself on his pyjama trousers, which he found softer.

The lack of harmony between the couple grew more marked, to Lamine's consternation.

'Ousmane, what are you doing to that girl? You don't want a wife. It's a slave you need. Try to change: "commune with your spirit", on your pillow. You will see where you are in the wrong. This is what African wisdom advises.'

But for Ousmane, any compromise was synonymous with surrender. He countered Mireille's 'stubbornness' with 'the hardening of his own position'. Even when he was in the wrong, he would not give in. Any compromise, any backing down, seemed to him the abdication of his own personality. He laid into Lamine unsparingly in his turn: 'You don't realise that you are betraying your true self. You live like a *Toubab* you think like a *Toubab*. If it weren't for your skin you wouldn't be an African any more. You know you're deserting our ranks, just when we need trained men.'

Instead of taking offence, Lamine laughed at his cousin's over-reaction.

'How can it change a person to sit at a table and eat steak instead of rice? What harm does it do me to spend my salary on my family instead of subsidising a lot of idle parasites? And if to respect my wife and let her live happily in the way she chooses means that I've been colonised, well then, I've been colonised, and I admit it. I want peace. That doesn't mean I'm a traitor to myself.'

'That's not the point,' Ousmane argued. 'The things you mention are trivial aspects of your behaviour. But you know perfectly well that the way one behaves governs the way one thinks. What you are losing is enormous. It's your African soul, your essence as an African. And that's serious, very serious!'

Mireille listened to this conversation in consternation.

Part Three

1

Ousseynou had complained one day in front of Mireille, 'I'm always the one who comes to see you. The fact that I'm not married is no reason why I should be the only one to make the effort. A friendship rests on two feet. One foot doesn't hold out for long.' And he gave his characteristic good-natured chuckle.

Mireille backed him up. 'Ousseynou is right. You must go and visit him.'

And Ousmane promised to drop in on his old neighbourhood.

The next day Ousmane drove out to Usine Niari Talli in his new Peugeot 504. His nostrils were assailed by the same nauseating effluvias borne on the evening air, as of old. Drains overflowed with foul, stinking water from the basins and buckets of slops emptied throughout the day. Ousmane cleared his throat, restraining a desire to vomit.

In spite of this, he smiled as he alighted, shaking hands with those who recognised him. Children rushed towards him. His mother's former neighbours surrounded him with words of welcome: 'Gueye! Gueye! Be in peace only, Gueye!'

He finally shook off the affectionate curiosity and entered the Ngom compound, after a long, emotional gaze at the hut where he had spent his childhood.

Ousseynou's father congratulated him. His wives greeted him warmly. And the banknotes with which he had come prepared, were distributed among the excited groups. They thanked him, they flattered him, they prayed for the good son who had grown up to have everything he could desire.

'We were sure that God would reward you, you were always so attentive to your mother's needs.' And the wagging forefinger of the right hand emphasised the words.

Ousmane smiled. The happiness which he brought made him forget momentarily the smell of dried fish, while he thought to himself, 'I did well to renew the contact. This is my return to my roots.'

Ousseynou wanted to receive him in the room which he had had built for all the boys in the compound.

But old Ngom invited Ousmane into his own room, which was

103

reserved for distinguished guests. A huge bed occupied the place of honour in the middle of the room. The coat-rack was collapsing beneath the weight of garments hung on it. In one corner a pile of sheepskins bore witness to the head of the family's piety, as did a collection of prayer-beads and a mass of Koranic books.

Ouleymatou served drinks. They talked of the past, recalling their childhood street-battles, the times when they had danced through tropical storms in search of any stranded motorists, whose cars they would offer to push, to earn a few pence.

And their wrestling-matches, when they were nimble youngsters in loin-cloths, their legs anointed with oil, and strings of talismans tied round their heads to impress their opponents. And their faces covered with cabalistic signs, traced in flour or charcoal.

And how the sound of the tomtom would accompany every match! Little girls would chant refrains to egg on the wrestlers. And provocations and challenges rang to and fro. Young developing muscles swelled with pride. They would take their courage in both hands. They would wriggle out of their opponent's grip. Legs would be twined round legs. At last the stronger or the more adroit would bring his opponent to the ground. And, while the vanquished lay sprawling, the victor proudly walked over to the drummers, to the accompaniment of the applause. He would raise his arms in the air and arguments from the supporters of both contestants would add to the noise and confusion.

In this way, all the youth of the neighbourhood had a cheap and harmless outlet for their high spirits, which helped them to forget the dust and noise and privations of their daily lives.

Ousmane laughed at these memories. He was reminded how he had been beaten by Ousseynou, but how he, in turn, had got the better of Seydou Niang.

He took to the wheel of his car again in something of a daydream. He could not get Ouleymatou's image out of his head now that he had seen her again. He had learnt from his friends, not without some pangs of jealousy, that she had been married off to an elderly cousin who owned a modern fishing fleet at Ouakam, on the outskirts of Dakar. They had split their sides in merriment at the expense of the elderly husband, whose scratched face told all and sundry that his young wife refused him his conjugal rights. A few months later, he heard, with subconscious relief, that she had returned under her father's roof. Ouleymatou's divorce had been the cause of passionate arguments among the group; some of them decrying forced marriages, others praising reason and wisdom as a guide in one's life.

'It may lack the spice of passion, but a forced marriage is capable of survival!'

This turbulent interlude in Ouleymatou's existence had left no mark on her beauty. Ousmane drove out her smiling image by concentrating on his wife's blonde beauty and the green sparkle in her eyes.

Ouleymatou, for her part, had also seen Ousmane again. She realised the truth of Ousseynou's words when he had described his friend as more flourishing than ever. Witness the gleaming new car . . . This visit definitely confirmed Ouleymatou's changed attitude to Ousmane, which had first manifested itself at the time of his early scholastic success, but which the young man's indifference had discouraged. Ousmane had made a real success of his life, whereas she had stagnated, badly nourished, badly housed, having to be satisfied when she needed clothes with her mother's rare hand-outs.

'Ousmane has become a real man,' she thought with bitter regret.

The *Toubab* wife, of whose existence she was aware, did not stop her. Nor did she hesitate on account of the baby, born a few months ago, and whose baptism had aroused much gossip. Ouleymatou was ambitious and she was in love. The difficulties in her path only increased her intent. She considered ways of renewing contact with Ousmane.

'We'll see,' she said to herself.

Her first move was to dismiss firmly her numerous suitors. She scorned them all as incapable of setting her up in the opulent style favoured in films. The screen had given her a taste for fine furniture, cars, tiled bathrooms, rustling gowns.

'What can Samba the butcher do for me, standing from morning to night in front of a stall that's worth less than five thousand francs? Or Diawara, the bus driver, traumatised by the financial demands of his employer?'

Ousmane was the only one for her. She was tortured with regrets. What an idiot she had been! Reacting like a child! But that child had now been trained by contact with experienced women; she had made a note of all the artful dodges that her elders evoked amid hearty laughter.

The ironic comments on the baptism of the half-caste child were a clear indication of Yaye Khady's disappointment.

'A baptism without any exchange of gifts. Poor Yaye Khady! This *Toubab* is a bitter blow for her.'

The first move in Ouleymatou's gambit was easy. She counted her trump cards. She was not averse to sharing. Sharing a man was the common lot of women in her circle and the idea of finding a man for herself alone had never crossed her mind.

She had a certain amount of education and her mirror paid tribute to her desirability. From every point of view, she concluded, she deserved to be the wife of a 'top dog'.

One day, as if by chance, she turned up at Yaye Khady's house. 'I happened to be in this neighbourhood, visiting a friend. I remembered you lived here now, so I dropped in to greet you.'

As Yaye Khady, who was busy with the ironing, showed her into the sitting-room, she added slyly, 'What! You're doing the ironing! At your age! What about your daughter-in-law? Can't she do it for you, if maids can't manage to iron starched materials properly?'

Yaye Khady burst out laughing. 'My daughter-in-law! Hasn't your mother told you? She's white! And for a white woman, the only person who counts is her husband. So I do the ironing. Your father, Djibril Gueye, is fussy about his boubous. Fortunately he doesn't wear them often.'

Then Ouleymatou took off her own boubou and hung it on one of the wires in the courtyard. She tucked her pagne up around her waist and without another word took the iron out of Yaye Khady's hands.

She sang as she ironed: the garments slipped sparkling from her hands. She folded them and placed them in a pile on a chair in the sun.

By noon, the basin of washing was empty. Yaye Khady could not believe her eyes: she ironed so quickly and so well, better than she did herself.

Yaye Khady thanked her and slipped money for her fare into her hand. But Ouleymatou protested energetically, 'From you to me, Yaye Khady! No! You are my mother. You have a claim on me. If I have nothing else to give you, I can at least give you my "sweat". I have neither husband nor child. I only do the cooking when it is my mother's "turn", and that's only two days in eight.

I'll drop in regularly and pick up Papa Djibril's boubous. I'll be delighted to wash them for you.'

She left without having mentioned Ousmane, who nevertheless filled her thoughts and sustained her zeal for ironing.

And once a fortnight Ouleymatou came and collected Papa Djibril's boubous. She always managed to find Yaye Khady alone. She refused to take the piece of soap that Yaye Khady slipped between the clothes. She backed away quickly when Yaye Khady offered her money for charcoal and for her busfares.

She was happy to help. Because she was in love, she felt herself capable of doing the washing for the whole household. But she wisely limited herself to Djibril Gueye's clothes. He blessed her endlessly:

'May God turn your fatigue into happiness, my child!'

Ouleymatou acknowledged inwardly, 'True love is the gift of oneself to the beloved, but it is also the gift of oneself to the beloved's parents and friends.'

Her mother encouraged her. 'Yaye Khady . . . an exceptional woman . . . full of *soutura* . . . She deserves "your sweat".'

Yaye Khady was indeed 'full of *soutura*'. She had often discreetly lent her money to eke out the budget of the compound, when her 'turn' fell in the middle of the month and she was obliged to 'borrow' condiments that she could not afford to buy . . . She remembered unpaid debts that Yaye Khady did not remind her to pay back . . .

She repeated, 'Yaye Khady deserves "your sweat" . . . She is very understanding, full of *soutura* . . .'

The mother's advice reinforced the daughter's attentions.

Ouleymatou washed and ironed. She wanted Ousmane and through Yaye Khady she would find the means of getting him back.

2

Ouleymatou worked out in her mind a detailed scheme to seduce Ousmane who progressively came to occupy the main place in her heart and thoughts.

One afternoon when it was not her mother's 'turn', and when she had already taken Djibril Gueye's clean laundry back to Gibraltar, she spent an unprecedented time over her bath.

One of her sisters, astonished at the unusual time she took over her toilet, remarked teasingly, 'Why, I see you've still only got two legs and one head! I thought you must have grown a double, from the age you've been in there, scrubbing yourself!'

Ouleymatou simply smiled. In different circumstances she would have put her half-sister in her place with a bawdy rejoinder, since, like every girl who grows up among co-wives and half-sisters, she was known for her sharp tongue.

She was adept at the insidious rebuke that made her many bitter enemies; she was skilled in the art of adapting proverbial sayings to new situations. Nothing could stop her when she had got it into her head to demolish or ridicule her opponent. Her half-sisters and stepmothers went in fear of her tongue.

It was said of her, 'She's got spirit. She defends herself like a tigress.'

And they said besides, 'She didn't do well at school. Her type of intelligence is the kind that understands mischief. One can't be queen at home and at school simultaneously.'

And, 'She's a real she-devil' . . .

But for once Ouleymatou smiled at her sister's teasing, instead of biting her head off. With more serious things on her mind than a squabble, she simply snubbed her, 'I've no time to waste with you.'

In fact she had only an hour—if her father's clock wasn't slow as usual—to catch Ousmane Gueye as he left work.

Her younger brother, who was one of Ousmane's pupils, had innocently let her know their timetable: 'Every Tuesday afternoon we have an hour's lesson with Monsieur Gueye.'

And Ouleymatou mused, 'To catch Ousmane at his work!'

She smeared a scented salve over her whole body till it shone and her oiled skin clothed her like a velvety film, which followed the swellings of her small firm breasts, curved over her hips to cover her firm, rounded buttocks.

Clouds of incense rose up from a clay vessel and spiralled round her parted legs; she offered her whole body to its warm, fragrant caresses.

She took strings of white beads from a box and draped them tinkling round her hips. She chose a pagne of light material, transparent enough to suggest her curves, while still remaining decent. She unfolded a new white bra that she had bought specially to emphasise her bust.

She tied a little *gongo* powder in a piece of muslin and slipped the sweet-scented aphrodisiac between her breasts.

Then, using all her skill with cosmetics, she powdered her face, applied mascara to her eyelashes, shaved her eyebrows which she re-drew faintly with her eyebrow pencil. With a brown lipstick she emphasised the outline of her mouth. She sprinkled a few tantalising drops of 'Sabrina'—the currently fashionable perfume—under her armpits and between her breasts.

As she moved, a gauzy boubou allowed a glimpse, now of a plump shoulder, now of her breasts in their lacy prison, now the strings of beads, standing out round her hips.

She slipped on a pair of red babouches which emphasised the black colouring of the henna with which she had tinted her feet.

She picked her way with care down the road to avoid stirring up the sand.

She passed Mother Fatim, her father's first wife, who looked at her suspiciously. She mollified her with, 'I'll be back soon. I won't be long.'

At the crossroads she hailed a taxi and, in a voice faint with emotion, directed the driver where to put her down.

Ousmane Gueye was holding an open book . . . And she could catch the sound of his voice.

She controlled her emotion and walked on as naturally as she could. She slowly reached the door of the classroom and leaned against the wall.

'I've come to see how my brother is getting on, with an eye to his exams.'

'Oh, very well, indeed,' said Ousmane. 'The pupil will soon be as good as the master. He's excellent.'

Ouleymatou laughed. Ousmane's nostrils were greeted by the tantalising scented exhalation that accompanied her movements.

In the courtyard he took in the whole picture: skin that gleamed like watered silk in the sunlight, black designs traced in henna glimpsed against crimson shoes, plaited hair beneath the wings of the knotted headtie, eyebrows arched over the seductive gaze, full lips with their expression of deliberate indifference. The scent of incense mingled with *gongo* rose from the folds of the visitor's garments. Ousmane's eyes wandered with desire from her ample bosom to the curve of her hips, from her plump little bottom to her smooth armpits. He undressed her in his mind, down to the black ribbon around the little white petticoat clinging to her skin. Ouleymatou talked to hide her emotion. She asked after Yaye Khady; she asked after the white wife and the newborn son. She pretended not to notice Ousmane's confusion.

Ousmane was shaken to the depths of his being. Suddenly he felt desire surging through him, breaking like surf against the professional ties which kept him prisoner at that moment.

He gazed at Ouleymatou. Ouleymatou gazed at him. There was mutual embarrassment and Ousmane held out his hand as naturally as he could. 'I must go back to my class.'

Ouleymatou smiled. 'Of course. But give me something to pay for a taxi. I have a claim on ''your sweat'' as Ousseynou's ''hut brother''.'

'That's true. Here you are. Excuse my oversight. I should have thought of it.'

'Thank you,' and Ouleymatou picked her way daintily across the school yard.

When she was a respectable distance from the high school she opened her right hand. There she saw a crumpled blue banknote. She unfolded it and smoothed it out.

'A ''blue''! My sweet little ''blue'', I'll make you good as new,' she sang to herself.

Ironically she said to herself, 'Djibril Gueye, your son is paying handsomely for the laundering of your boubous . . . All the same, your wife shall get one thousand francs . . . And one thousand shall go to my mother!'

The rest? She saw herself in a pink boubou, contrasting with her black body. Ousmane Gueye will see . . . If he can hold out till his next visit, promised for a month's time, to avoid any suspicion.

And then, she wasn't a woman for nothing! She had noticed Ousmane's embarrassment, and the slight tremble in his voice had not escaped her. His haste to leave her betrayed his confusion.

She had been right to believe, 'Allah! Allah! *Bèye sa tôle*. Cultivate your own field. God helps those who help themselves.'

After this graceful, scented apparition Ousmane Gueye had great difficulty in concentrating on the essay he was correcting. An inner turmoil distracted his thoughts. He could scarcely control his agitation.

That evening he did not wait for Boly, the colleague and friend to whom he gave a lift home every Tuesday.

He found his wife busy with their child. He took the baby from her and put him in his cradle. Then he took Mireille in his arms and in the body of his white wife assuaged his desire for the black woman.

He was thrown off his balance by her sexuality. There was invitation in that little white pagne reaching to mid-thigh, in those tinkling rows of beads to be fingered in the dark, in the tantalising scent of *gongo* and the titillating whiffs of incense.

Ousmane Gueye dreamed . . . And Mireille was subjected to onslaughts which she did not provoke. These repeated erotic exercises did nothing to cure his obsession. He was relentlessly teased by his overwhelming, ever-present desire for the black woman.

Ouleymatou had an unexpected opportunity to visit the school sooner than she had anticipated. Her younger brother had been taken to hospital with food poisoning and her father sent her to inform the school authorities.

The pink boubou produced the desired effect.

'Pink and black!' Ousmane Gueye exclaimed. 'Is that the way you dress up to announce that your brother's ill?'

'Me! Dressed up?' she protested. 'Father was in such a hurry to get me out of the house that I barely had time to wash my face. You know what Papa Ngom is like. When he gets an idea in his head he won't give anyone any peace.'

And she burst out laughing. Her laughter and lissom movements under the gauzy boubou set the strings of beads tinkling round her hips. The scent of *gongo* arose from between her pointed nipples.

Ousmane's blood coursed through his veins. In spite of his

111

marriage and his philosophical studies, he still remained an unbreakable link in the chain forged by atavism.

A toothpick lodged in the corner of a mouth or artfully shifted over tattooed gums, braided hair falling around the black oval of that face, the languishing look in those huge eyes, those graceful movements, the rustle of a boubou loosely floating or held in check by studied gestures: the powers of Eve's seduction worked their magic and all his resistance fell to pieces.

What could Mireille's lack of sophistication do in the face of the provocative tinkle of beads around the hips, or the aphrodisiac potency of *gongo* powder? What could Mireille do against the suggestive wiggle of an African woman's rump, wrapped in the warm colours of her pagne?

He had struggled to forget Ouleymatou's seductiveness. He had tried to cure his obsession by bedding his wife. But what could Mireille do against the law of the blood?

Defeated! Ousmane admitted that he was defeated. His life had been one long battle: against poverty, to come first, to escape from Coumba's clutches, to win Mireille.

Must he go on struggling? Must he start all over again? Must he stand firm? His whole being said no. His conscience was strong enough to fight to the end, to win still more victories. But he no longer wanted to resist. He wanted to live, to live at last.

Ouleymatou did not know what to expect. Would she be summarily dismissed like the last time? Or? . . .

Ah! Ousmane was no longer frowning. He let the tide of love flow over him. He held out his hand and imprisoned that of Ouleymatou. His hand was warm, quivering with controlled desire. Ouleymatou vibrated at this contact. Their eyes met. And it was Ouleymatou who withdrew her hand with false modesty.

'I've things to do at home!'

'Not so much that you can't cook me a nice fish couscous for my dinner,' retorted Ousmane. 'I like it well spiced with not too much tomato.' He opened his wallet and rifled through its contents.

'Another "blue"!' Ouleymatou thought.

'This should cover your expenses. Don't forget to put in Oba and Yaboye,*' Ousmane added.

'I know you adore them,' said Ouleymatou. 'But look out for

---

* Two kinds of deep-sea fish of a particularly delicate flavour but very bony.

the bones! Have you forgotten the day when Ousseynou got one of the little bones stuck in his throat?'

'No, I've forgotten nothing,' Ousmane replied enigmatically.

He had, indeed, forgotten nothing.

With a light heart Ouleymatou set off home through the two noisy thoroughfares, sure of her victory.

3

When she got back to Usine Niari-Talli, Ouleymatou delightedly showed her mother the blue banknote.

'Ousmane Gueye is eating here this evening. Ask Aunty Awa to look after my little sisters. You've got your "turn" with father, so you'll be out of the way.'

Ouleymatou took off her pink boubou. She bought bleach and soap powder and set about scrubbing out her mother's bedroom. 'The *Toubabs* are so clean,' she said to herself, and she didn't want to be found wanting in this respect.

She rubbed and polished and shook out and smoothed down. She put a clean white sheet on the bed. She placed the incense burner in the middle of the room. She sprayed each corner with eau de cologne to freshen the air. She closed the door.

She took some couscous from her mother's store-cupboard, added water, mixed it to a smooth paste and put it to steam in the couscous steamer.

At the nearby market she selected two pieces of Thiof*. In these she made three deep incisions into which she placed a stuffing made of parsley, chopped onion, garlic, chilli, bayleaf and salt, blended in a mortar. Large red tomatoes were added to thicken the sauce in which cassava, pieces of white cabbage, carrots, turnips and a slice of pumpkin were already cooking.

The couscous was swelling up and softening in the steam. Ouleymatou tipped it into a saucepan and broke up the lumps. She crushed powdered baobab leaves in the mortar and added these to make it more glutinous, then put the mixture back into the steamer which was waiting on the fire.

Like an expert cook she rapidly dipped her right forefinger into the boiling pan and tasted to check the seasoning of the sauce.

She reckoned up what she had spent and reported to her mother, who was watching her, 'I've got four thousand francs over.'

'Give them back to him this evening,' her mother advised, from the depth of her experience. 'As the saying goes, "If you want a lot, take a little". It'll make a good impression.'

---

* A deep sea fish whose flavour is much prized by Senegalese.

Ouleymatou went to the shower-room. She rubbed and scrubbed her body all over with a well-soaped loofah.

Ah! Her body! She groomed it, she polished it, she perfumed it. She took every care of it, for it was her weapon of seduction.

She had wasted enough of her youth hanging around the old women. All her contemporaries had got married, one after the other. With or without encouragement, they had accepted their first suitor. Her own short-lived marriage had sent her back into the ranks of the spinsters.

It was high time she quit these ranks, once and for all, to enter the grown-up world, according to her dreams.

She dispatched one of her young brothers to engage Mabo, the neighbourhood musician. 'Tell him I'm expecting a distinguished guest.'

When Ousseynou came home he found Ouleymatou radiant.

'Who are you entertaining? A minister?' he teased her.

Ouleymatou shook her head.

'No. Just Ousmane Gueye.'

'Who?' Ousseynou asked anxiously. 'Say that again.'

'You heard me. Ousmane Gueye. He asked me to make a couscous and invites you to share it with him.'

Ousseynou inquired indignantly what Ousmane Gueye, the husband of a white woman, was doing in their compound, and if their mother knew what was going on.

Ouleymatou nodded. 'Do you think that's funny or improper or extraordinary? Tell me.'

'Neither funny nor improper nor extraordinary,' Ousseynou corrected her. 'But I'm telling you to watch your step, sister. A white woman doesn't share her man. Honour demands that you refuse to be Ousmane's plaything. He's my friend. It would be a serious insult to me, an unforgivable shame if Ousmane played fast and loose with you and then didn't marry you. If Ousmane comes here just to amuse himself, if instead of setting you up, he degrades you, if you're just an object to him, it would be a serious matter, very serious, you understand?'

Ouleymatou understood. She had already turned the matter over in her mind, hundreds of times. But what could she do? Fate had linked Ousmane inseparably to her heart. Her will had become the pawn of her passion and the tool of her ambition. Ousmane now represented her ideal. For years he had been the only man she found worthy of her virginity, jealously preserved for the awakening to the sound of the tomtom, the morning after her wedding night. Her rather free and easy behaviour had led her many suitors to try to break down her resistance by force or by guile. But she had always managed to sail intact through the troubled waters of desire, until her marriage. Now that she had already given proof of her virtue, no-one could hold her back any more.

She yielded unquestioningly to her love. She was a woman, she was in love, she was adept in the art of seduction and laid her traps to realise her ambition and assuage her passion. What concern of hers was Ousseynou's 'dignity' and 'honour' and his long-standing friendship? What is more, who could tell what the future held in store? Some *Toubab* women had shared their husbands, or had quit Africa, driven away by African women. Ouleymatou was no fool. She knew how to play her hand. Her mother had reminded her of the saying, 'When you want a lot, take a little'. She declared, 'When you want a lot, you must give a lot.'

A dinner for men only, to found a teachers' association, was the pretext Ousmane invented to explain to Mireille his evening's absence.

'They'll call on the women teachers later on!'

And to make this last-minute dinner sound credible he had grumbled, 'What a bore it'll all be, everyone imagining himself radiating brainwaves. If only I could get out of it!'

And with a worried look, feigning annoyance, he had showered and dressed. He planted two kisses on his wife's cheeks and raced downstairs.

His arrival at Niari Talli was greeted by the whole compound. Ouleymatou's mother, prudence personified, advised him to park his car at a neighbouring petrol station, which he did.

Old Ngom, seated on his sheepskins, responded to his greeting with a tinkle of his prayer-beads. Ousmane Gueye had a smile and a generous gesture for everyone.

He thus promptly spelled out his intentions.

The force which drove him on admitted neither secrecy nor ambiguity. What animated him came from his heart, his mind, his reason, and demanded nobility.

Ouleymatou showed him to the bedroom. He was greeted by swirling incense and stepped back, the better to confront it. He sank down on the bed, without waiting to be invited. But he knew he could permit himself this licence. The boldness of the gesture, according to tradition, better than any words, revealed his intention to marry.

His body seemed to float with the swirling incense. And Ouleymatou busied herself with serving the dinner.

She wore a tightly fitting camisole, nipped in at the waist and stopping suggestively at her hips. The generous décolleté revealed her quivering bosom. Her buttocks bobbed up and down under the folds of her pagne. Her arms moved with ease and grace.

Ousseynou, who had by now recovered his good humour, came to join his friend. Ousmane's significant round of greetings, which excluded any idea of a hole-and-corner affair, had allayed his annoyance. Ousmane was not up to any devious manoeuvres. In any case, had Ousmane ever been known to be devious?

The unmarried girls from the neighbourhood compounds came to share the couscous. Ouleymatou had invited them to give herself some publicity and finally dash the hopes of the males who were sniffing round her.

Everyone sat around the dish—the women on the floor, the men on benches and cushions. Ousmane had taken off his jacket and hung it on a coat-rack.

He refused the spoon he was offered. He experienced a childish pleasure to be eating with his fingers again. He kneaded a mixture of fish, vegetables and couscous into little balls and chewed them slowly. The hot chillies stung his tongue, brought tears to his eyes and made his nose run so that he had to hold his handkerchief to it continuously.

Ouleymatou teased him, 'You were the one who asked for a highly spiced couscous!'

The women picked out the choicest titbits for him, the guest of honour, and piled them up in front of him.

He thought of the formal ritual of his *Toubab* meals: plate, fork, knife on the right and not on the left, little spoon for coffee, medium sized spoon for dessert, large spoon for soup.

And Mireille always scolding him, 'You used the wrong spoon.'

Here, the 'right spoon' was the hand. And nobody had told him, 'You forgot to wash your hands.'

Here, the right hand was dipped into the dish, selected a suitable morsel, scooped it up, kneaded it, dabbling about in the sauce amidst chatter and laughter.

Ouleymatou's caressing voice urged him, 'Eat, daddy!* Eat! It's all for you!'

Then, in an undertone, 'Eat, Oussou!'

'Oussou!' Yaye Khady's voice at his window in the mornings when he dozed on, too lazy to get up. Oussou? Warming himself by the fire in the cold dawns, doing homework by the light of a storm lantern. Oussou? A father's anger at some prank or at the sight of Yaye Khady embracing him with excessive affection. Oussou? It meant his love for Ouleymatou, his adolescent's heart tortured by a girl's rejection.

Oussou! This one word awoke his past, which now returned to upset his present!

Oussou! Ouleymatou soothingly murmured over and over, 'Oussou eat, eat! Oussou, drink! Oussou, wash your hands! Oussou! Oussou!'

And Oussou ate. His palate delighted once more in hot chillies and the flavour of his native dishes. His eyes were moist, his forehead perspiring; he was happy. It is true, he had forgotten these strong sensations of African life.

Ouleymatou placed a calabash of water and a piece of soap in front of him, then eau de cologne to get rid of the lingering smell of fish.

Gradually the other guests slipped away.

When they were alone Ouleymatou drew the curtain. Then Mabo Dialli, the *griot*, began strumming on his Khalam. And as he plucked at the strings his voice rose up in warm cadences:

'Oussou, prince of culture!

But before you were a prince of culture

You were and are a Lebu prince.

A white woman forsook her country to follow you

But better than the white woman

The Black girl is worthy of you

Look, look at Ouleymatou, your sister by her blood and by her skin.

She is the one for you.'

He was lulled by the harmonious plucking of the strings. How many inflexible wills, how many heroic resolutions have been

*Senegalese women never call their friend, lover or husband by his first name out of politeness.

overcome by the notes of the Khalam!

'Diali, Diali!' sang the young black woman. 'Unsettle his senses, trouble his heart, Mabo Dialli. Help me to seduce him. I advance towards him. Neither a knife at my throat nor a wall of flame can stop me.'

Ousmane heard this protestation of love, this cry escaping from the depths of a soul, and addressed to him.

'Unsettle his senses, Diali! Trouble his heart!' And he melted like a lump of karite on hot coals. He was tense with desire.

He drew Ouleymatou unresisting towards him. The Diali put on his slippers and discreetly disappeared. He had already pocketed on his arrival a thousand-franc note to pay for his services.

4

From now on Ousmane found himself caught up in a double life. Gradually he replaced his European suits by more comfortable caftans. He shared his leisure time, in equal stints, between his wife and his mistress, whose parents pretended to be unaware of what went on in the bedroom behind the closed curtains, and condoned the liaison.

Ousmane Gueye had the support and good wishes of the whole compound. The gargantuan meals he provided, the banknotes distributed, the attentions lavished on all and sundry, stifled any ill-will.

Mother Fatim, Pathé Ngom's first wife, an unfailing critic of the loose behaviour of the girls in the neighbourhood, for once had nothing to say.

Money silenced the voice of her conscience. She had no wish to kill the goose that laid the golden eggs. She was even of the opinion that Ousmane was on the lookout for a wife and the best means was to get Ouleymatou pregnant. 'Then the white woman would be faced with a fait accompli.'

Pathé Ngom, sunk in his prayers and his rosaries, was unaware of the truths that were circulating in whispers.

And it was Mother Fatim, the figurehead of the compound, who slipped Ouleymatou incense and aphrodisiac powders at night, with a knowing wink.

Ousmane Gueye's frequent absences finally broke up the atmosphere of his home. Mireille was crushed by loneliness and torn between anxiety and jealousy.

Ousmane's former passionate lovemaking was now followed by almost total abstinence, which he attributed to fatigue.

'They don't leave me time any more to spend with my wife. Setting up this Association takes all my free time. That's the price you have to pay when people rely on you.'

'That's a lie!' Mireille snapped. 'Three months! It's too much! You're never at home! You've got a mistress.'

Ousmane denied this.

But his wife was sure he was deceiving her. She had no idea what her rival looked like or what her name was. But she was in no doubt of the existence of a rival, who was stealing her husband from her every evening. And she was black; the heavy persistent smell of that detested incense lurked in Ousmane's clothing.

Mireille had made every possible concession, she looked after him, showed hospitality to his parasitical cronies, demonstrated her good will; but nothing could hold Ousmane any more. Every evening he left his home to join his mistress.

Night after night passed. Incense rose in clouds. They feasted on highly spiced dishes, nostalgically reliving the kingdom of childhood. Mabo the Dialli plucked at the strings of his Khalam. The whole compound flourished at Ousmane's expense.

In the Gueye's flat silence replaced their former quarrels. What is left of a couple when they no longer share their meals? What remains of a couple when they no longer share in chatter and discussions? What is left of a couple when lovemaking deserts their bed and its sheets remain unrumpled?

Painful questions in Mireille's head; deep suffering in her flesh. Ousmane had no time to see the effects his absences were having on his wife. Nothing in his home interested him. Absent-minded and detached, he countered his wife's nervous, anxious state with insolent silence. He could hear the call of 'Oussou!' in his heart, and hurried off to Niari Talli. 'Oussou!' The nickname linked him to his past and sang to him of his future.

Ouleymatou had become his true soulmate, the woman in whom he recognised the extension of himself. She was, as Mabo Dialli so rightly sang, at one and the same time his roots, his stock, his growth, his flowering. They were linked by their childhood, spent in the maze of dusty streets. Most important, they were linked by their common origins: the same ancestors, the same skies. The same soil! The same traditions! Their souls were impregnated with the sap of the same customs. They were excited by the same causes. Neither Ousmane nor Ouleymatou could disclaim this common essence without distorting their very natures. Cultural heritage was taking its pitiless revenge. It was reclaiming its due and revealing to Ousmane the end-point of his flight.

And Ouleymatou started vomiting and went on vomiting, and it was common knowledge that she was expecting a child. Her 'Oussou's' child.

Mixed marriages will always occur: white men legally endowed with black wives; black men often sincerely committed to a marriage with a white woman.

Ousmane associated with some mixed couples. Certain of his friends, who had been married longer than he, disapproved of his marriage, in spite of their own similar choice.

'We chose this way during the colonial period, out of self-interest, laziness, weakness or opportunism. But you! With the rebirth of our country and the evolution of the black woman! You were the black woman's hope!'

Ousmane listened and watched. Some of these men—out of self-interest, laziness, weakness or opportunism, to quote their own words—had let themselves become shamefully assimilated. They had put up no resistance. Their wives had taken upon themselves to manage their husbands' lives and had reduced them to ciphers. They introduced into their homes the mentalities, customs and habits of their own countries, completely submerging their husbands' cultural traditions. The man was out-and-out European-ised, mercilessly cut off from his origins. 'Wretched puppets!' Ousmane grumbled. There was nothing of the African left to them except their skin. Their children were brought up as little white kids, boasting names like Ralph, Arthur, Melanie, Isaure! Monsieur did the shopping, the cooking, the washing-up. Monsieur pushed the baby's pram. But the worst of it was the barrier that Monsieur put up between his home and his parents. Everyone spoke French with a Parisian accent and neglected their native language. When the children of these marriages grew up they would become the harshest and most contemptuous racists. 'This cross-breeding impoverishes and exploits Africa,' thought Ousmane. In Ousmane's eyes, this cross-breeding was not to be advocated.

In the case of certain couples, the African man asserted himself and commanded respect for his origins. His wife adopted his life-style, having agreed to this arrangement. The rights of the family were recognised and respected. The children were named Malick, Badara, Fatou, Yacine. The children wore national costume. They had no objection to eating with their fingers. They mixed with all the children of their own age and thought of themselves as Negroes.

'That type of cross-breeding enriches Africa,' Ousmane thought.

Elsewhere tolerance reigned with respect for their differences. The couple lived without friction. When the time comes, the children are free to choose where they belong.

That was the type of home that Mireille had dreamed of! Between the two extremes, it would have been easy for Ousmane to create such a home, since his wife, while retaining her own personality, did not attempt to make him her slave. But, when all was said and done, was Ousmane really interested in the peace and equilibrium of his household?

With time, the fickle nature of his erstwhile commitment became more and more evident. A clear-headed analysis of his feelings revealed his true love. His allegiance to Ouleymatou had been the reason for his refusal to indulge in casual affairs. No woman could take her place.

Mireille? He admitted to himself that he had been drawn to her by the need to assert himself, to rise intellectually and socially. 'The European woman's qualities, her spellbinding beauty, the attraction of the unknown, a taste for originality . . . all these strengthened the links that bound us!'

He searched and searched . . . He searched and found many a tributary to swell the torrent of passion which carried him away.

His self-scrutiny revealed a commonplace truth: he was deceiving his wife because he no longer loved her. He made love to the black woman because he was happy to rest his head on her plump thighs. Then Ouleymatou's fingers caressed and stroked his hair, gently sliding her fingers over his scalp, teasing out the minutest scales of dandruff.

5

When Mireille gave birth to a fine boy with amber-coloured skin and curly hair, Yaye Khady had suffered to see the infant's resemblance to the son of her 'blood'.

This had struck Ousmane too. Tomorrow would not his son find it hard to forgive him for condemning him to live on the fringes of two worlds destined never to mix? However strong the maternal influence, this child would never be fully accepted in the white world. He was bound to be conspicuous at all times.

However charitable and tolerant his own world might be, his son would only be accepted and welcomed affectionately, on condition that he reconcile himself to being black. But while he was young he would first have to endure his schoolmates' inconsiderate teasing: in spite of his Senegalese name, Gorgui, they would make fun of his hair and his colour, shouting 'Coffee-coloured! Coffee-coloured!' after him.

Yaye Khady had picked up the child. Her pinched lips betrayed her dissatisfaction, whereas Mireille, reconciled to her choice, was radiant in the joy of motherhood.

Djibril Gueye had drawn himself up to his full height. Holding the infant in his arms he had made up for all the wrongs by his words: 'This is one of God's creatures; he is born of parents chosen by God and will become what God wishes.'

Ousmane had insisted on a quiet baptism for his son. The naming ceremony of *Toud* had taken place in his tiny flat, without any of the usual ostentatious display.

El Hadj Djibril Gueye had arrived with his fellow Muslims. He had been the star of the ceremony, both officiant and godfather. Yaye Khady had at least taken the trouble to dress the little Gorgui in his finest pagne.

The men walked one by one up to the baby's cradle and placed their little finger in his right ear, while murmuring his name. They had recited prayers for the child's brilliant future, 'between his father and his mother', along the royal path that leads to God. Mireille looked on.

But Yaye Khady was appalled. She had dreamed of the feasts that marked family ceremonies. But all her hopes had been dashed, first by her son's marriage, celebrated secretly in a foreign land, and now this baptism.

Some of her female relatives and women friends had found her speechless with grief. She had voiced the problems which beset her. 'A white woman brings nothing to a household. Who am I going to exchange greetings and gifts with? The baptism of a firstborn son should be a grand affair, the talk of the town. But this day is sadder than a day of mourning.'

The relatives and friends had sympathised with her. Some of them had been quite pleased to take back the pagnes and the thousand francs that they had probably borrowed to help Yaye Khady fulfil her obligations. Others had launched into a profusion of comforting words that deceived no-one. Yaye Khady knew that no sooner had they crossed her threshold, than their jeers would flow freely. They would exclaim, amid bursts of laughter, 'What! Is it a baptism or a funeral?'

'Wherever do these young people go to hunt for wives?'

'A baptism without the ritual exchange of pagnes and gifts?'

There was great dismay in Yaye Khady's heart.

A few months after this baptism that was impressed on Yaye Khady's heart as a disgrace and a mortification, a delegation composed of Ouleymatou's three stepmothers and three of their neighbours from Grand-Dakar, set out for Gibraltar. Yaye Khady had been notified the day before to expect them, and racked her brains for the meaning of this visit.

She had no inkling of her son's nocturnal expeditions to his former neighbourhood, nor of the torments of his infatuation.

In spite of her dizzy spells, Ouleymatou continued to take charge of Papa Djibril's laundry. Yaye Khady had indeed guessed at her interesting condition. She had observed her cheeks losing their colour, her features becoming drawn, the blue rings around her eyes. But in her wisdom she had not voiced her suspicions. She was a thousand miles from suspecting who was responsible for the physical changes which she noted.

Nobody had had the courage to tell her about her Oussou's liaison. The virtuous Yaye Khady and her husband, a soldier of God, would certainly have considered their son's intrigue unworthy of a married man, and have put a stop to the affair, so depriving a whole compound of manna from heaven.

Mother Fatim, the senior member of the delegation, was the first to speak, after interminable exchanges of greetings and the offer of refreshments.

'When one finds a fruit, it is necessary to ask questions. Your son Ousmane has sown his seed in our daughter Ouleymatou. Does he accept the "fact of God"? Do you accept the fact of God?'

Yaye Khady was taken by surprise. She pondered for a moment, silently admitting to herself, 'Any African woman rather than this white woman. Any African woman would show respect and consideration for me. God is sending me a child to bring Ousmane Gueye back to the right path.'

Aloud she said, 'Ouleymatou is my daughter as much as yours . . . As a little girl, she was always helpful to me, and still is. Her mother is an elder and of good counsel. If another boy had wronged her and refused his responsibilities, and Ousmane had been designated to put the matter right, he would abide by the decision. There's no need to beat about the bush. We shall do our duty. But I cannot promise marriage. Ousmane Gueye must make up his own mind. We shall also need to consult Djibril Gueye.'

'Djibril Gueye, El Hadj, will look favourably on the marriage which will make reparation for the wrong done by his son,' Mother Fatim objected.

Soukeyna served more drinks. To gain time, the visitors put the bottles of sweet iced liquid to their lips and sipped slowly.

Three crisp, new thousand-franc notes offered to Mother Fatim, the spokeswoman, closed the interview.

'To pay for a taxi,' Yaye Khady explained.

'Peace and Peace! Thank you for your hospitality. We shall know what to say when we are asked about our mission.'

And the visitors rose to their feet.

Once outside the house their tongues were loosened. They exchanged comments on Yaye Khady's attitude.

'She's delighted with the event, which will distress the white woman.'

'And she'll have a grandchild who'll come up to her expectations.'

'*Thieye Yallah!* Heavens above! She welcomes the child so that she can get back what she's laid out on other people's ceremonies. She'll make up for the depressing baptism of the *Toubab* child.'

One voice enquired curiously, 'How can one be the mother-in-law of a white woman? I wouldn't like to be in Yaye Khady's shoes.'

One woman commented enviously on the improvement in Yaye Khady's status. 'She puts us in the shade; she's not one of us any more. Did you see her sitting-room? An educated son certainly brings financial returns. The drinks came out of a refrigerator, and I caught sight of an electric iron.'

'Yaye Khady has remained unspoilt, hospitable, courteous,' Mother Fatim interrupted tartly. 'May God preserve her.'

Ousmane did not deny that he was the father of the child. He admitted to his mother that the love he now felt was stronger than his love for Mireille.

'One dreams of something. One fights to obtain it. One sacrifices everything for it, and once you possess it, it is no longer enough.'

Ousmane unburdened himself. He needed the friendly ear of his mother to get everything off his chest. He needed to tell of the agony he had suffered and how he had given way to temptation. He had been deceiving his wife for months. He was worried about his double life. But he was happy.

Yaye Khady listened. 'What do you intend to do?'

'I am a man of honour. Ousseynou, my "hut-brother", lives in that house. I shall not inflict shame on him by evading my duty. I will marry Ouleymatou on condition that she agrees to receive me when it suits me. She will not have her "turn".'

Yaye Khady warned him, 'That is against religion. A wife must have a "turn".'

Ousmane explained, 'I have looked into it. If the wife accepts her husband's suggestions, then there is no sin. Ouleymatou can choose and will have the last word.'

He left, partly relieved of the burden which had weighed heavily on his conscience for months.

And his mother rejoiced . . . Yaye Khady rejoiced once more in her existence.

Ouleymatou gave birth to a son, and Djibril saw in the child's sex the sign of God's will.

'Ousmane must get married. One does not abandon an heir. God gives his blessing to the marriage.'

Djibril Gueye sent a delegation of co-religionists to his former neighbour's compound, to ask for Ouleymatou's hand.

'Mireille is a Muslim,' he said. 'She knows that Ousmane has a right to four wives.'

Yaye Khady was overjoyed. At last she would occupy the place of honour at a ceremony which she would organise, of which she would be the prime mover and, what is most important, from which she would derive material benefits.

She despatched a band of devoted *griotes* to every part of the town: a rapid conveyor-belt of news, set in motion by the quantity of bank-notes soon to be distributed. Through their voices Yaye Khady bade her sisters, female cousins, women friends, acquaintances, relatives, former and present neighbours, attend the great gathering of the eighth day.

An impressive number of women, in bright array, set forth to hand over to Ouleymatou's mother the *rouye*, money to defray the costs of the baptism.

Yaye Khady generously allowed all her women friends to demonstrate the gifts of money properly donated on these occasions, Ousmane having acceded to all his mother's demands.

'A righteous man must honour a woman who has given herself to him.'

And Ousmane, with repeated withdrawals, depleted his bank account.

And crisp new banknotes dazzled Ouleymatou's parents.

'Fifteen thousand francs in compensation for Ouleymatou's virginity, although Ousmane was not the first!'

'Ten thousand francs for new clothes to wear at the baptism ceremony.'

'Five thousand francs to help the mother-in-law to meet her expenses.'

'Ten thousand francs for food for the new mother.'

And the biggest bundle of all! A hundred thousand francs! For the costs of the actual baptism feast: millet, lunch, lamb roasted on a spit, drinks, ginger beer, etc.

The spectators' breath was taken away. Yaye Khady's *griote* concluded her peroration:

'My noble patron asks if everything is in order. Ouleymatou is her daughter. She wishes Ouleymatou to be radiant. Ask and it shall be given to you. Ask and you shall be obeyed.'

One old woman murmured, 'There's still three thousand francs wanted for candles to light the young mother's room.'

The *griote* immediately proffered the sum.

Ouleymatou's mother delegated her jeweller to voice her thanks.

'Ouleymatou's labour pains have not been in vain. A woman must give herself to a man who recognises her worth. The eye of Ouleymatou, illustrious beyond measure, has encountered the gaze of an eye even more illustrious. Yaye Khady has not disappointed my noble patron, for even if the money comes from the pocket of Ousmane Gueye, it is with the consent of Yaye Khady. I thank all the Gueye family. Djibril has recommended what God preaches for two people who love one another: the union of marriage.'

Ouleymatou's mother wept with joy. The onlookers applauded. The *griotes* danced, intoxicated with the characteristic odour of new banknotes.

'The baptism will bring in a nice round sum!' And Usine Niari Talli was already buzzing with the promise of festivities and display.

6

The long-awaited day finally dawned. Yaye Khady was getting her own back on Dame Fortune. She had tinted her hands and feet with henna. An expert hairdresser had plaited black sisal fibres into her hair, in an elaborate coiffure.

The morning? The routine business of a baptism: the men despatched to give the infant his name, calabashes of *sanglé* to be prepared, the packets of fritters ready for distribution, amid laughter, jokes, teasing, happiness on everyone's face.

In the afternoon, the women flocked to the Gueye's house. They overflowed from the tiny courtyard onto the pavement and under the marquee erected over a green lawn. In one evening trampling feet would wreak havoc on the labours of the gardener to the housing estate.

With so much money changing hands, who could distinguish the rich from the poor in the parade of brightly coloured, silky boubous, in the display of golden jewellery?

Yaye Khady checked the arrivals, separating the sheep from the goats. She singled out those who had helped her when the white woman's child had been baptised. The ones who had laughed at her then did not smile now. They agreed that Yaye Khady had gained in respect. They couldn't put a figure on the number of women who had accepted her invitation.

From all sides Yaye Khady received money and pagnes, basins of rice with meat or fish, bowls of fruit, dishes of barbecued lamb, in return for identical gifts that she had made to all and sundry on similar occasions.

She was the focal point of the gathering. Would anyone like some ginger beer? Some cakes? Did anyone need a glass? Everyone was jostling to get served.

She resisted the griots' entreaties to collect her guests together and set off for Grand-Dakar in a procession of taxis and coaches, all with hooters blaring.

She was returning to her old neighbourhood as one enters a conquered territory. For this once-in-a-lifetime occasion, she was adorned from head to foot in more than five hundred thousand francs worth of jewellery and garments. The bracelet on her right wrist alone was valued at three hundred thousand francs.

Her new neighbours escorted her in style. Long gold chains hung down from their necks. Wrists were encircled with bracelet upon bracelet. To make a more lavish show, they had recourse to the jewellery of more affluent friends. And they strutted, laughing and gesticulating, while taking good care not to be robbed of finery that did not belong to them.

Marième, Coumba's daughter, carried the basket of gifts, as was the custom. A *gor djïguène*, one of those persons of ambiguous sex, whose existence revolved around similar ceremonies, watched over the infant's hamper, in which were piled up baby clothes and toys and carefully folded pagnes which the child would eventually wear.

Yaye Khady advanced, followed by her retinue of friends. Her *griote* sang loudly to catch the attention of the crowd: 'You are not the most ill-favoured, nor the most tight-fisted.

'Ah! Behold my princess! She advances like a *Linguère*, a noble lady of yore. You, the descendant of Lat-Dior Ngoné Latyr Diop, show Usine Niari Talli who you are. Your ancestor courageously refused to submit to the white folk.'

Yaye Khady advanced. Her black and green boubou was raised to show her fine, gaily-coloured pagne, woven by the famous Mandjaque weavers.

'Yaye Khady, Usine Niari Talli has an illustrious hostess. May the grains of sand, may the leaves of the trees retain the memory of your visit.'

The *griote* gesticulated, pointing Yaye Khady out to the whole assembly.

'Your retinue is the symbol of your greatness.'

And the procession advanced, amid an uproar of applause, people pushing, jostling, falling over each other to get to the front.

Ouleymatou's mother smiled at her guests. She had set a marquee aside for them. Benches and chairs sagged beneath their enormous thighs, weighed down with layers of pagnes.

They formed a circle, with Ouleymatou's mother and female relatives on the one side, facing Yaye Khady and her escort. The specialists in the protocol associated with the exchange of gifts stood in the middle.

The spokeswoman for Ousmane's family took the initiative, as was correct:

'Five hundred francs! The first donation from the father's family!'

'Two thousand francs! For the soap and mat to shave the infant!'

'Two thousand francs! For wood to light the young mother's room, from the husband's nephews!'

'Two thousand francs! For the young mother's maternal and paternal aunts!'

'A thousand francs! For the young mother's personal *griots*!'

'A thousand francs! For the young mother's first cousins!'

'A thousand francs! For the young mother's family jewellers!'

'Ten thousand francs! Second donation from the father's family to the new-born child!'

The *griotes* handed over each donation, preceded by the ritual expressions of greeting and gratitude, wishes for peace and long life, not forgetting invocations to Allah, the master of man's fate. Ouleymatou's family, when their turn came, doubled the sums they had received, and returned them.

The traditional exchanges drew to a close. These did not involve very large sums. But scarcely were they concluded than they were followed by other exchanges which this time would effectively impoverish the young mother's family.

According to the traditional system, the financial interests of the husband's female relatives are never seriously endangered. They gamble enormous sums, often borrowed for the occasion, which the other camp—their dignity at stake—must lose no time in doubling.

The clamour of Yaye Khady's arrival had left no doubt about her intention to ensure that the exchanges were on a grand scale. Her suitcases were lifted down from the taxis and coaches and opened.

The spectators were dazzled by their rich contents.

Yaye Khady's *griote* proclaimed, 'Eight pagnes and a hundred thousand francs! The gift of Ousmane's sisters and female cousins to their nephew.'

The announcement was greeted with applause.

Four elegant boubous were ostentatiously thrown into the laps of Ouleymatou's mother and three stepmothers. That intended for Mother Fatim, the senior of the three, was wrapped in a pagne!

A blanket was unfolded. The patient workmanship of a Malian weaver, its originality took the onlookers' breath away.

The *griote* gave voice again: 'This blanket is offered by Yaye Khady to Pathé Ngom! To preserve him from the cold! Was ever the head of a family more greatly honoured?'

Drumsticks pattered on tomtoms to express satisfaction as the voice died down; then it was raised again with the cry, 'Paternal and maternal aunts of Ouleymatou! Yaye Khady honours you with fifty thousand francs!'

Tirelessly the *griote* announced gifts of banknotes, pagnes and boubous to all the members of the Ngom family. Women who could claim only the most distant relationship or connection by marriage had been unearthed for honouring.

Finally Yaye Khady addressed the lower-caste women who inhabited her former neighbourhood. Each generous offering was preceded or else followed by a hubbub and jostling, praises and thanks.

'Those who have laboured in the kitchens' also received 'the soap' which will wash their clothes.

The onlookers expressed their keen appreciation in a storm of cries:

'Yaye Khady has an all-encompassing eye.'

'Yaye Khady has acted on a grand scale.'

'Yaye Khady has done everything.'

It was the turn of Ouleymatou's family to reply. They doubled every sum that they had received, as well as every object. For months, her mother had had a quantity of pagnes woven in anticipation of this ceremony and had stored them in trunks. She was prepared to lose a lifetime's savings in one evening in order to come up to expectations. She was acclaimed in her turn, as woven pagnes and boubous of damask and Lagos cotton were heaped up in front of Yaye Khady.

The tomtom expressed the onlooker's satisfaction. Applause broke out accompanied by cries of delight.

The *griotes* danced into the middle of the ring, loosening their pagnes to free their legs. They stamped their feet, swung their hips, threw out their arms, in time to the excited beat of the drummers.

One of the dancers revealed a wooden phallus sticking out from her loosened clothes. This unexpected apparition was greeted by a frenzied uproar which drowned the drums.

Then came the rush forward with outstretched hands. Appetites had been sharpened by the rain of banknotes. The spongers pushed and jostled in a free-for-all. Every woman was either abused or flattered in an attempt to relieve her of the last coins in her purse.

Yaye Khady stood her ground, against all the pushing and shoving. She clutched her handbag to her chest and shouted as loud as she could, 'I will distribute everything that I've received, for everything that I've received must honour this great day. But I don't live here. I shall discharge my responsibilities from my home in Gibraltar.'

Sharp-eyed friends packed the new acquisitions into the suitcases and loaded them onto the taxis and coaches.

With the same hooters blaring away, the group drove back to Gibraltar where, amid uproar and commotion, the pagnes, boubous and money were once more shared out, to be followed by distribution of the barbecued lamb.

In spite of her fatigue, Yaye Khady was elated! At last she had had 'her day of glory among her peers!'

Those who had been present at this spectacular function would put a stop to any future slander; they would display the proof of her financial resources and restore her dignity . . . She was happy and invigorated and the fires of shame that had burned her up during long sleepless nights were finally extinguished.

'*Santa Yallah! Santati!*

Thanks be to Allah! Give thanks again!

Give thanks that the black blood in the veins of the new grandson is not diluted; this child who will give back what it has received to the source which gives him suck!

Give thanks for a daughter-in-law at last who will respect my rights!

Santa Yallah! Santa rêque!

Thanks be to Allah! Give boundless thanks!'

And Yaye Khady exulted . . .

Ouleymatou's mother, too, exulted. The neighbourhood had witnessed, with her daughter's function, a unique ceremony, with an abundance of food and a 'ballet of the banknotes' that no marriage or baptism could equal.

She was elated, with no regret for the savings that had melted away or for her trunks left empty. Her labours were bearing fruit. On her daughter had been bestowed the accolade of 'wife of an intellectual!' 'The equal of a white woman in a man's heart!' Her daughter had been honoured far above her elder sisters.

In Usine Niari Talli Ouleymatou was admired: a suitor's moral qualities carrying little weight in people's judgements, money alone

134

being at the heart of their raptures over Ouleymatou, merchandise that had gone to the highest bidder! The women sang Ousmane's praises as 'financially solid', 'the open-handed Ousmane'! They praised heaven for having sent them a young and charming son-in-law, a *goro* of noble birth, with flourishing finances and one, moreover, who was 'their own son', 'a better man in truth, far better, than the man from Ouakam'.

In reckoning up the pros and cons, Mireille scarcely came into the picture. She was the intruder to be eliminated, the rival to be dethroned, in a word, the outsider . . .

Everyone thought, 'What's she doing here, anyway?'

Against this chorus of recriminations, Ali and his wife tried to redress the balance: they tried to breach the wall of hostility that Ousmane erected as soon as the question of Mireille was brought up.

Ali grumbled, 'So, the best-laid theories crumble as soon as they are faced with life's realities. Those who formulate them most fiercely cut a pretty poor figure when it comes to carrying them out!'

Ali had been surprised at first. Now he was revolted. Ousmane Gueye, the most 'intellectual' of their group! Ousmane Gueye, the uncompromising disciple of 'Negritude', who used to advise them to 'open up', was now turning in on himself, with the excuse of not betraying 'his roots'!

'Words and phrases have no value unless they are put into practice, and then people often abuse and distort them!' Ali thought. 'Should one despair of mankind? Man has a heart and reason, which are the basis of his undoubted superiority. Ousmane is no longer making use of either!'

Ali often cast his eyes around the globe and let his thoughts linger on countries that he had visited or that were still unknown to him, those washed by oceans or clinging to the sides of mountains: 'Man is everywhere, whatever his language or his colour.

'It is all a question of learning to let one's heart beat to the rhythm of the universe! Of accepting that the time will come when frontiers will be banished and all are united in one grand dialogue! And here is Ousmane repudiating everything he stood for, all because of the "white skin" he introduced into his home . . . My voice? One weak sound in the symphony of the world . . . My aspirations? As well try to sweep away the ocean! But my hopes remain immense! A day will dawn when nobility, nourished by universal values, will overcome reluctance and prejudice!'

135

Ali cornered Ousmane. 'There's such a thing as a code of honour. I'd say the same thing if you had betrayed a Senegalese Alima or Oumou. You are the cause of a woman breaking with her own family, and by creating factors for her isolation you don't help her to integrate with a new environment . . . Mireille is not a mistress. Even a mistress would have her rights . . . She is your wife, a wife creates obligations. And you refuse her your regular presence! You make use of her property in the most despicable manner. You seem to have lost every virtue. You are beyond the pale of the religious morality that your father taught. Beware of the avenging hand of God!'

'Stop!' Ousmane objected. 'You're not telling me anything I don't already know. But when you want to judge a situation properly, you've got to look at it from all sides. Here, on the one side, is Mireille, her rights as a wife, the burden of her exile. All right. But, in your argument, what do you do about Ouleymatou? Her dignity would suffer if I abandoned her. You are forgetting her family. They would be covered with shame if I dropped them. Ouleymatou has a son . . .'

Rosalie interrupted tartly, 'Mireille comes before Ouleymatou! If you had married Ouleymatou, we wouldn't be here arguing about her today. She waits till you are married to hook you! What a scenario! Her attitude is unworthy of a modern woman. Women should stick together.'

Ousmane said seriously, 'I love Ouleymatou, that's the important point. I realise now that she has always been the only woman I have ever loved and that I never stopped loving her. What about Mireille? What was I trying to prove? My manhood? My ability to attract someone so far above me? I was excited by the difficulty of the enterprise. Once I had reached my goal, I felt the immense void that separates me from Mireille. When I rediscovered Ouleymatou everything became clear. The truth may seem outrageous. You want me to respect a commitment which no longer satisfies me? Must I give up living so that I don't deceive anyone? Must I drag out my days instead of living?'

Ali's earnest expression indicated the exceptional circumstances.

'You alone are to blame, you're the only one responsible. You don't engage the future lightly. You should have thought more about it. This woman asked nothing of you, imposed no conditions. On the contrary, she has given you everything. Pay your debts.

Have the courage to repay. Repudiate Ouleymatou.'

Ousmane could scarcely contain his anger.

'That's easy to advise. It's easy to talk of duty. But where does my duty lie in this case? In abandoning Ouleymatou and my son? In erecting a barrier between my mother and myself? Then I'd have nothing left to live for.

'If I went back to Mireille, how could I make her happy if I had no heart in it? The present situation helps me to put up with her. I'm hoping that with time . . . One day perhaps . . . Many things work out with time.'

Ali lost patience with such words. Could it be possible that Ousmane had been bewitched? In his distress he considered that his friend was 'lost to honour', that honour that they had both previously defended so obstinately.

7

While Rosalie was doing her best to distract Mireille from her melancholy brooding, Ousmane Gueye had already installed his new family in a house large enough to make a home for his mother-in-law and Ouleymatou's brothers and sisters, which hid from the neighbours the identity of the real mistress of the house.

He had taken the precaution of warning them, 'There will be no "turn". I shall come when I can. I shall never spend the whole night here. But Ouleymatou will want for nothing.'

In the face of Ali's repeated attempts to lure him back to his true home, Ousmane remained disappointingly obdurate. The upheaval in the life of his best friend left Ali at a loss. Rational man that he was, he again began to think of the possibilities of a spell having been put on him by some marabout. Might Ousmane not be the victim of the *dédélé*, the spell by which a woman in love makes a man grow fond of her?

'Could be! It could well be!' Rosalie sighed.

Might not Ousmane's soul have been hidden in a horn and buried on the seashore, to make it inconstant, like the ebb and flow of the waves?

Could be! It could well be!

Might not Ousmane's soul have been hung up in a doorway, in a talisman, to bring it hurrying back to his African wife?

Could be! It could well be!

In a state of agitation, Ali caught up with his friend as he was coming out of school. Ousmane was on his way to Ouleymatou's.

'Don't drive off. Listen to me a minute.'

'Still the same subject?' Ousmane asked.

'Alas, yes,' Ali replied. 'Friendship has its obligations. No matter what respect one owes to one's parents, the fact that you find yourself siding with Yaye Khady in this problem is a clear indication how wrong you are. What Yaye Khady believes in can't be right for you. How can *you* subscribe to your mother's ideas and her ridiculous taste for extravagant ostentation? How can *you*, Ousmane, betray trust? I hardly know you in your new guise . . . Besides, what do you reproach your wife with? Her colour? Her mentality? The same grievances that her father had against you?

138

Ridiculous! So you are the racist now . . .'

Ousmane listened. The voice of friendship sounded reasonable. But how could he describe his daily battle between his emotions and his reason?

'You're not telling me anything I don't know,' he said. 'I'm still the same person I always was. But a man is a complicated mixture of aspirations. And it's difficult to combine all the conditions for his fulfilment. I realise that I have in Mireille a wife who loves me. But when I'm with her, I have a depressing feeling of dissatisfaction, of something lacking. Then things began to go wrong . . . added to this, there is the mutual antagonism between my wife and my mother . . . the misunderstandings between Mireille and my friends—except for you, naturally, you stand up for her—but all the others who, to use her own words, ''violate our home''.'

Ousmane was silent for a moment. He shook his head.

'You've got to reckon with the force of habit,' he went on, 'the force of beliefs that you can't escape from, without uprooting yourself. The weight of the past is a determining factor. I can't manage to find myself in Mireille. There's something I'm craving for that she can't give.'

Ali remained unconvinced. 'And yet Mireille can understand many things. It's you who are trying to complicate things. You are trying to find cultural justifications for what is simply a physical infatuation. You think that a silly girl like Ouleymatou, who didn't even finish primary school, can contribute any positive guidance in your life?'

'But she knows the legend of Samba Guéladio; she knows our proverbs. We can communicate by a remark, a greeting, a glance, and that's important,' Ousmane answered. 'We have the same time-honoured terms of reference.'

'In a cloud of incense and *gongo*,' Ali mocked, 'while counting the beads round her hips! Just use your commonsense; I'm convinced that you're making a complete fool of yourself. You've got to get her out of your mind.'

'How?' asked Ousmane, his interest aroused.

Ali now took command. 'Tomorrow, you've got the day free? . . . Right. Wait for me outside your house at six in the morning . . . Agreed?'

Ousmane, half-seriously, agreed.

Ali watched the car drive off in the direction of the house rented for Ouleymatou. He shook his head sorrowfully.

As they drove along, Ousmane sat beside his friend, lost in thought. Ali was perhaps right to be so hard on him. Perhaps supernatural powers had been released without his knowledge and were making him hate the person who had been the object of all his dreams, whom he had striven for for five long years. Had some force worked on him to make him obsessed with Ouleymatou? Had she had recourse to some marabout's spell to revive his youthful love—the length of white twine into which they patiently knot their incantations while reciting the name of the person to be bewitched? The hardest heads are said to be unable to resist this test.

Or had signs been scribbled on two halves of a sheet of paper, which had then been thrown in opposite directions, to separate him from Mireille?

His irritation with Mireille and the lack of affection which he showed to his half-caste son were not normal.

The experiment that Ali suggested was worth trying, all the more so as a childhood memory persuaded him to have faith in traditional practices.

Mother Fatim, Pathé Ngom's first wife, ruled the household like a tigress. She ran a food-stall at the open-air market of Nguélao, in Grand-Dakar, and the riches she thus acquired, added to her position as 'Awo' or senior wife, allowed her to make exaggerated use of her prerogatives. Her co-wives feared her viper's tongue which could distort the most harmless facts and turn every situation to her own advantage. And, in particular, she would get the head of the family, who was always inclined to take her side, to hurl abuse at her adversary.

How many new wives had packed their bags, repudiated by Pathé Ngom, because Ma Fatim said they had been rude to her? One newcomer, Maïmouna, had sworn to dig herself in the compound so that she could not be dislodged. And, if one day she were to return to her family, Ma Fatim would not be the cause of her repudiation. Maïmouna was on her guard. She took care not to cross the 'old lady's' path, to that she could not be accused of 'impertinence'. She never made use of any of Mother Fatim's utensils, even if they were left lying about in the courtyard, as if to tempt her.

When Maïmouna swept, she cleaned thoroughly everywhere, taking special care to sift the sand in front of Ma Fatim's door.

She filled up her water-jars for her every day, during her frequent absences. She offered to cook for her, when it was her 'turn'.

Maïmouna's mother had warned her, 'The path to peace is short. Act towards your elder as you act towards me.'

But it was difficult to escape Ma Fatim's spitefulness. She always found something to criticise: there was sand in the couscous, or it was too salty, or not salted enough, there was grit in the rice which hadn't been properly sorted, or else it was the fish which wasn't fresh and which 'would poison the whole compound'.

Maïmouna calmly put up with all the criticism, while the other wives looked on mockingly. The presence of guests increased Ma Fatim's malice.

Ousmane recalled one Thursday. He had been at the Ngoms' when Mother Fatim came back from the market about midday.

Her gaze went straight to the clothes line where Maïmouna's freshly starched clothes were hanging.

'Who has hung those clothes there, in place of mine? My clothes may be old, like me, but I set store by them.'

From her room Maïmouna could hear the provocation. But Yaye Khady, who was visiting her, signalled to her not to go out and to keep her mouth shut.

Then Ma Fatim planted herself in front of her young rival's door, shouting, '*You* dared take *my* clothes down from *my* clothes-line and put your own up in their place? What cheek!'

Maïmouna handed her the pile of clothes, neatly folded. 'They were nice and dry and warm when I took them down.'

Ma Fatim's hand pushed away the pile of clothes and landed a couple of resounding slaps on Maïmouna's cheeks, with all the strength of her hatred and black ingratitude.

Maïmouna fell back. To the physical pain was added surprise and shame. The many occasions when she had put her courage to the test in avoiding confrontation, were interpreted by this old fool as weakness! She had put up with her tongue-lashing and her snide remarks, all for nothing! What! She was wearing herself out, doing double work, instead of getting any rest, all for an ungrateful wretch of a woman! Ma Fatim didn't deserve any respect. Like the ex-wives, Maïmouna was going to show her what's what!

She stepped back and then hurled herself at Ma Fatim's skirts. She lifted her up by the shoulders and threw her violently onto the ground. Yaye Khady was too disgusted to intervene immediately.

She gave Maïmouna time to plant her fat bottom on the old woman's shrivelled chest and to return with interest the couple of slaps she had received.

Only then did Yaye Khady shout, 'Come quick!' They're fighting.'

But it was clear that there was no fight. Only Maïmouna was hitting out. Ma Fatim's white hair was full of sand and had lost all the talismans that usually adorned her head.

Strong hands were needed to detach Maïmouna's fingers that gripped her co-wife's scrawny neck.

Ma Fatim was freed, but she still lay motionless. Her children carried the inert figure to her room. Her eyes were open and rolled back so that only the whites were visible.

Her sister, called urgently from Pikine, gave her diagnosis. 'A *rab* has possessed her. You know perfectly well that if an angry *rab* hadn't interfered, Fatim could have smashed three Maïmounas. Fatim has been neglecting the *rab* and devoting all her time to her business and he's getting his own back. We'll have to organise a *ndeup* to appease him.'

Family councils and argument followed. The Iman intervened, forbidding this activity in the name of Islam; nothing could make Mother Fatim's family change their mind. To effect the old woman's cure, they demanded a *ndeup*, the exorcism dance.

On the appointed Thursday, from three o'clock, the benches set round the space intended for the pagan dance, gradually filled up. The bolder spectators pointed out the *ndeup* dancers.

Chanted incantations merged with the beat of the tomtoms. Mother Fatim was seated on a mat, her arms and legs stretched stiffly out, pieces of white string tied round her wrists and ankles. Her deep-set eyes gleamed under a blood-red garland. Since she had hidden herself away, her cheeks, now daubed with soot, had grown hollow and her jaws protruded. She crossed and uncrossed her spindly legs in an attempt to keep up appearances, to a chorus of praise to Mame Coumba, the Queen of the Waters, and exaltation of the celebrated Fulani, the King of the Senegalese Plains.

There rose up an ever-increasing roar of exhortations, born in the night of time, from tormenting anguish and man's inability to find any rational explanation for certain events.

Among this crowd of onlookers, attentively following the proceedings, were certain persons to whom the duty of attending on the *rabs* and perpetuating offerings of flesh and blood, had been handed down by their ancestor, who had no doubt reddened the blue of the sea by festivals of sacrifice. The same ancestor who had doubtless shuddered with fear or thrilled with joy when the greedy waves licked at the blood shed at his feet. He had listened to the voices of the deep and found in their wise gravity balm for his sufferings. Had his anxieties then melted away in the surging waters, and had strong gusts of wind carried his wishes away to be fulfilled?

Arms jerked upward in supplication to heaven. Women and men conversed with the Invisible. Their eyes were fixed on the same point, and the smile on their lips bore witness to some dazzling experience. Every gesture, accompanied by a particular resonance of the tomtom, was a message. The Perceptible and the Invisible were in communion. Souls quivered in a trance of possession, inspired by their familiar. And the tomtom muttered, muttered; the tomtom muttered, muttered, the catalyst for the intermingling of two worlds, the living world and the world of the imagination.

The mistress of the ceremonies was a toothless old woman, with a bird-like head and spindly limbs protruding from her multiple layers of clothing and amulets, which increased her size without impairing her ease of movement.

The possessed were called upon to answer 'present', and, as the eager chanting joined with the ecstatic pounding of the tomtom, they shuddered and fell into convulsions and trances.

Had they drunk too deep of the milk that the mistress of ceremonies had offered—the primary food of life and the favourite beverage of the jinnee? Or was it the relentless, monotonous, persistent beat of the tomtom, wearing away the consistency of the soul?

Or the soporific chanting voices, drowning anxieties and distress?

The dancers' heads grew heavy, they collapsed on the ground, rolling in the dust, and fell into a deep sleep.

'*NDeuk! NDeuk! NDeuk!*' proclaimed the chorus.

'*NDeuk! NDeuk! NDeuk!*' replied the tomtoms.

The royal *Back*, of the Lord of all the lands and seas together, echoed, '*NDeuk! NDeuk! NDeuk!*'

The vast extent of Cape Verde in all its beauty at his feet!

'NDeuk! NDeuk! NDeuk!'

And every true-born Lebu! And Mother Fatim opened out her hands and smiled broadly as she answered him:

'*NDeuk Daour* oh!

143

Soubal nagnouma!
NDeuk Daour oh!

The dyers have honoured me!

The whole gathering was caught up in the rapid beat. Heads and torsos swayed in a collective intoxication.

All eyes were riveted on Mother Fatim! She waved her arms in the air. Would the miracle occur! Would she stand up? Would she walk? Had the *rab* been pacified? Would he forget his anger? Had he accepted the ox that had been offered? Was he showing the mercy that was hoped for?

In the dark and withered face of the 'patient', between the indigo lines tattooed on her gums, showed the gleam of a smile, still miraculously intact in spite of her years.

Hearts throbbed with hope. Hope swelled above the beat of the tomtoms. There was hope in the ecstatic gestures of unspoken prayer of the mistress of ceremonies. The sun deserted the sky, to add to the mystery of the occasion. A soft wind spread intoxicating aromas of iodine and salt. Eyes grew wide with curiosity.

Suddenly Mother Fatim's pitifully scrawny body began to vibrate and shudder. She smiled at the mistress of ceremonies who lifted up her garments and danced for her. She moved one foot forward, and then the other. The sound of the tomtoms gradually died down. Ousmane remembered being spellbound by the spectacle, as he perched on the roof of his father's hut with lads of his own age, an old cap on his head and holding on to his shorts which were too loose at the waist.

He recalled the sight of the crowd dispersing noisily. Mother Fatim, walking without support, zigzagged back to the Ngom compound. A few youngsters lingered in the twilight, kicking up the white dust. But they suddenly stopped larking around, at the thought that the spell might be contagious, and, more important, at the thought of the hiding they were likely to get for coming home late, which would spoil their escapade.

Ousmane recalled other pagan ceremonies. But the most disturbing display was when the *rabs* were associated with religion. The introduction of prayers into these pagan dances was sacrilege. He had argued this in many a noisy discussion with his pals.

Slumped in the seat of the car, he let his thoughts dwell on his past. His gaze was lost in the morning mist, pierced by illuminated shop signs and the headlamps of vehicles.

8

Ousmane was quite sincere in agreeing to get involved with ancestral healing practices, which are also said to help in strengthening will-power and bringing people back to the straight and narrow path. But his reason had difficulty in finding its way amidst the tangle of tradition and custom.

He hoped to return to his adolescent mood when everything was simple, including Mireille.

'If there is a choice to be made, it ought to fall on Mireille. Mireille alone, but, without any unkindness . . . what about Ouley-matou? If I find myself in this dilemma, it is because of her.'

He was ready for any suffering, if suffering could cure him. But could he exist without the ecstasy that Ouleymatou meant to him? His thoughts reverted to Mother Fatim.

'Was the *ndeup* responsible for her cure? Had the popular support and the atmosphere engendered by the chanting and drumming overcome the weakness of her legs? Had her paralysis simply been simulated, to explain her defeat? Did *rabs* exist, guiding our destinies according to their whims, bringing joys or misfortunes?'

He remembered scraps of conversation with friends who had studied medicine. In the psychiatric department of the Fann Hospital, they made much use of the *pinth*, the general assembly under the palaver tree, which approximated to group therapy, and of the *ndeup*, the exorcism dance. They also relied on the skills of the *bilodja*, sorcerers who used to have the power to kill.

Another aspect of 'African Science' which would make Mireille smile . . . 'The past and the present inextricably intertwined!' Not having the power to separate them, Ousmane imagined demoted jinnee and *rabs*, dislodged from their caves, dancing round a gigantic fire, while sorcerers flourished their feather garments.

The car drew to a stop at Fimela. The two friends were surrounded by jostling market-women, offering to sell them red chickens, the colour of palm oil, an essential element of the purifying bath at Simal.

Ali had explained, 'We are going to Simal. My father once took me there.'

145

They asked their way of one of the women, who pointed out the path they had to take. Deep ruts worn away by wheels, indicated that the road was in constant use. A woman who was sorting a bundle of old clothes for sale smiled at them. A man driving a horse and cart obligingly pulled up to let the car pass. Then they came in sight of the officiant's domain: a stretch of grey water enclosed by bushes, in front of which, a natural setting, screened by three huge tree-trunks over which a mass of foliage twined, invited them to partake of its mystery. A white bird perched sleeping on top of a solitary stake that rose like a mast in the middle of the still pool.

The officiant, tall, black and gaunt, smiled on all and sundry, revealing his teeth stained red with cola. His clients waited patiently, seated on a rough-hewn bench, whose surface was polished by time and the service it had rendered. The space reserved for the 'consultations' was divided in two by a fence. The first half served as a changing-room. In the second and bigger compartment stood a fairly large tub, which some young girls filled with water; in this bits of wood were floating. Two benches faced each other, one reserved for the officiant, the other for the client. The gaunt man brandished the red chicken in his long arms, and struck the naked client with it, from his head to his feet. The chicken squawked its disapproval of this treatment, and then, laden with all the impurities of the person who had come in consultation, it gave one final cackle and expired. The officiant drew the gizzard out of the dead bird and spread its contents on the ground. From the form of the entrails he could foretell the future. A swelling in the shape of two horns indicated that Ousmane had been bewitched by someone, at whose beck and call he now was.

'A woman is bringing you bad luck,' said the scrawny man, adding, 'It's a good thing you came to me!'

To complete his 'cure', water was poured over Ousmane, soaking him from head to foot. He rose to his feet, feeling a sense of relief, and proffered a five hundred-franc note to his 'saviour'.

He got dressed again in the changing-room, while another man followed him to the consultant.

Seated on the dried leaves, facing the water that rippled in the light breeze, Ali and Ousmane both held in their hands one of the pieces of yellow wood from the tub, which prolonged the salutary effect of the bath.

'Thanks, pal,' said Ousmane. 'Even if I'm not "delivered", even if I don't get back my former self, I appreciate your loyal friendship.'

Ali replied, 'I had a choice of two places for you. The other one is called "Djam-Wally", which means "I greet you"; it's on the border between Senegal and Gambia, where a great disciple of Mouridism used to live.'

They got back into the car and Ousmane took the wheel. He drove with great care. The purifying bath had not driven Ouleymatou from his mind. He was troubled by the desire to see her. The need to hold her in his arms was overwhelming . . . He no longer saw Mireille as the goal of his desires.

Mother Fatim, who had been put back on her feet thanks to the *ndeup*, had been more fortunate than him.

That evening, when he had finished his classes, Ousmane did not go straight home. He drove along the corniche and then, feeling refreshed, stopped the car. He climbed over the rocks which separated the road from the sea. The sea! All he wanted was to gaze on it again, to watch the water rippling in the wind. The fresh air whipped pleasantly against his face and purified his lungs. With his hands dug into his trouser pockets he thought about his two wives and whistled softly.

They were both beautiful in their different ways. Both took a pride in their person and left nothing to be desired in this respect. Ouleymatou went to inordinate lengths to keep her house clean and tidy. She knew how obsessive whitefolks were about tidiness and did not want any comparison to her disadvantage.

Ousmane turned up at her place at all hours, bringing anyone he liked. He was sure to find a smiling welcome which put everyone at ease. When the family had finished eating, there was still enough in the enormous common dish to satisfy the appetites of any new guests as well as the young *talibés* who crowded into the courtyard, on the lookout for left-overs.

As far as Mireille was concerned, Ousmane had given up trying to get her to accept his cronies. In any case, the dainty dishes that she prepared with so much care never satisfied their stomachs, used to more copious fare. And the cronies preferred to meet him at Ouleymatou's.

He smiled. 'Mireille would have talked of wastefulness, although she's so rich! She thinks that here they encourage slackers and layabouts.'

At Ouleymatou's he was the lord and master. He undressed where he liked, sat where he liked, ate where he liked, dirtied anything he liked. Any damage was made good without a murmur. In this home his slightest whims were anticipated.

In the flat he had to watch his every step.

'Don't make a mess!' scolded his wife, wearing her apron. 'Since you don't help me in the house, the least you can do is to try not to give me extra work! Put things in their proper place!' she ordered, pointing a peremptory finger.

His dirty clothes had to be put in the right linen basket: the blue one for white clothes and the red one for colours. He frequently put things in the wrong basket and Mireille never failed to point out his mistake.

According to Mireille's strict upbringing, the only place for food was the living-room or the kitchen. The war on cockroaches had its rules! It was unheard of to nibble a piece of bread in the bedroom. As her husband's equal, she would challenge his ideas and decisions when these did not suit her. She considered she was his partner in the marriage. She would discuss matters on an equal footing. She honoured her obligations but she knew her rights and stood up for them. Certainly that did not displease Ousmane. But no man is averse to being the leader and having the last word. A man doesn't refuse the prerogatives he is granted . . .

The comparison favoured Mireille in the matter of the bathroom and the library. In Mireille's blue-tiled bathroom, shelves were filled with bath-salts and all sorts of refreshing liquids to dissolve in the warm water of the bath-rub. Towels, as large as a pagne and soft bath-robes waited, neatly folded on a stool.

At Ouleymatou's, there was only a shower-room, with no hot water, no tiling, which the whole family had to wait their turn to use.

As she had left school early, Ouleymatou did not possess a single book. Ousmane installed a few books on a shelf, as the nucleus of a library, hoping to interest her in reading.

Mireille had brought back from France trunkloads of books and papers, for which she had set aside a whole room. And Ousmane Gueye would remove a work to read, taking it back to finish at his black wife's place.

He stood on the bluff, still whistling softly, while the sea breeze played around him. 'Ouleymatou!' He acknowledged that by renewing his relationship with her, he had restored a link with himself. Two halves of the same seed, once more united . . . The seed would live again . . .

How could he explain that Ouleymatou helped his 'revival'?

'What help is Boly MBoup's knowledge of mathematics in the face of dreams and fantasies like mine? The situation is too insubstantial to be reduced to a formula and solved by an equation!'

He remembered a conversation they had had. He recalled Boly's melancholy expression, the gestures indicating his helplessness as he said, 'My family reproach me for having married a Catholic. But what else could I do when the parents of girls I was in love with refused to let us marry because I'm a *griot*? The majority of girls from my caste are not educated. They are steered in the direction of the kitchen. As far as domestic work is concerned, *griote* girls are champions! But they have no idea of the importance of a home. They leave the house unswept and neglect their husband and children, so that they can perform at functions that are the source of their income. But you are a pure-bred *guer*! Whatever made a high-caste man like you marry a white woman, when there are plenty of black women who are good enough for you? I warned you while there was still time. Certain types of behaviour are tantamount to throwing in the sponge and betraying other people's expectations. Any capitulation, any departure from the path you are following, is a betrayal. Frequently, when a black man marries a white woman, he is lost to his country.'

The last sentence of this friendly conversation struck him anew and motivated his fight. He strengthened his resolve not to 'Be lost'. He admitted that he would have done better to marry an illiterate black woman and help to raise her up to his own level than to be floundering around in his present dilemma.

He took God to witness: 'My meeting with the white girl was determined by Fate; my will, more than ever, influences me to retain my identity as a black.' His soul rejected the subtle process of being decanted into an alien vessel. How is it possible to mingle values of differing content and expression, that are often conflicting, contradictory even, frequently at variance with each other? 'An incompatible mixture!'

'Ouleymatou, the symbol of my double life!' Symbol of the black woman, whom he had to emancipate; symbol of Africa, one of whose 'enlightened sons' he was.

In his mind he confused Ouleymatou with Africa, 'an African

which has to be restored to its prerogatives, to be helped to evolve!'
When he was with the African woman, he was the prophet of the
'word made truth', the messiah with the unstinting hands, provid-
ing nourishment for body and soul. And these roles suited his deep
involvement.

Mireille, armed by centuries of civilisation, could survive, with
her iron will, her enthusiasm for a confrontation, and with her
immense fortune.

Ousmane rose to his full height. 'Must I back down because of
my white wife's anger? Because she may get violent in her fury?
Because, every day, my conscience hears a warning bell? Back down
because of the universal code of honour and dignity? Impossible!'
In his entanglement with Ouleymatou, far more was involved than
the mere physical relationship. When those gentle black hands
massaged his muscles with infinite tenderness, a deep affinity was
established. It ate into his innermost being, shook him to the core,
disturbed his very soul, and set him up as a 'fighter', an ambassador
of his people' . . . 'A people bastardised by history, a people whose
fractured skeleton had to be re-assembled . . . A people stifled in
tunnels of fear and humiliation . . . A people! Oh! I was led astray,
when I was a young student, stuffed with reading and slogans,
bewitched by the novelty of the siren-song that lured me on! The
trap-door opens up. I am escaping unharmed!'

While engaged in her domestic labours, Ouleymatou would sing
determinedly, '*Fi*, Mireille *doufi nané gneh*. Here Mireille will drink
no sauce.'

Ousmane interpreted this as '*Fi*, Mireille *warou fi nané gneh*. Here
Mireille must not drink the sauce' (the sauce being the symbol of
privileges, honours and well-being).

So his choice was that the white woman must go.

'Cut her off, among her own people. Let her eat her heart out
from neglect and boredom . . . Don't react to her everlasting fault-
finding. Make it easy for her to leave, and then there'll be no
ambiguity about the role I shall be able to play; I'll be guaranteed
a free hand . . .!'

Ousmane whistled softly. The last stirrings of his conscience sank
for ever into the sea, as the sun was sinking before him in crimson
and lilac streaks on the distant horizon, above the line of the dark
blue waters. A boat was sailing into the distance . . . 'Towards what
port? With what souls aboard, subject to what implacable hand of

fate? . . . Souls which today must make decisive choices that tomorrow will be repudiated.'

When Ousmane got back to the flat he had to change before going on to Ouleymatou's. His shoes were encrusted with mud and weed. He laughed to himself at the thought that he was supposed to scrape them on the rough doormat, before entering the living-room 'in a civilised manner'. He whistled softly, 'Down with all the rules and regulations! An end to the robot existence! Long live nature!'

9

Friendship has a more constant code of behaviour than that of love. Friendship can be stronger than the affection born of blood-ties. A brother and sister are not necessarily friends. Time does not leave its mark on friendship. Love can become exhausted by crossing stormy waters, and rarely emerges unscathed from such trials.

Soukeyna, the elder of Yaye Khady's two daughters, had adopted Mireille as a sister and a friend. In the friction between Ousmane and Mireille, she attributed all the wrongs to her brother, for friendship can also be biased. Soukeyna argued, 'Mireille has not been lacking in goodwill. But a white girl can't suddenly become a complete African in her habits. The African woman has been brought up in a specific environment to satisfy the needs of that environment. She can't claim any special merit for adapting easily to her in-laws. But Mireille! She should get the credit for having tried. Her efforts ought to have been encouraged. But Yaye Khady is offhand with her and makes fun of her attempts at reconciliation. She would have liked to turn Mireille into her slave.'

Soukeyna and her sister-in-law got on extremely well. In spite of Yaye Khady's disapproval, she used to spend her weekends at the flat. She helped Mireille to turn out a successful rice with fish, of which Ousmane's portion stood all day getting cold in a serving-dish, as he never arrived for meals.

They sat in the study, having long and difficult discussions.

As soon as Soukeyna learnt of her brother's double-dealing, she came to visit Mireille nearly every day. Shocked and offended as she was, she tried to alleviate the situation. She even dared to confront Yaye Khady: 'By your selfishness you're driving Ousmane to eventual disaster; and simultaneously, you're killing another woman's daughter, as Mireille also has a mother. I am completely opposed to my brother's second marriage and consider that nothing can justify it except your self-interest. I'll have nothing to do with this second home. Mireille has attempted the impossible to try to please you! She even offered to take a turn in cooking at the brazier in the yard, to give you a rest, but you just laughed in her face. You discourage any attempts at co-operation. You reject her without even knowing her. Why? Because she's white . . . Her colour is the only reason you've got for hating her. I can't see anything else you can have against her.'

Yaye Khady gave her daughter a withering look. She couldn't believe a daughter could be so impertinent. She had heard that children today no longer respect their elders. Other people had spoken about it! But to listen to such impudence from her own daughter, and at her own expense! She wasn't having any of that. She would put this insolent miss in her place, her place being that of a child who has no right to interfere in grown-ups' business.

'Who asked for your opinion, you little snot-nose? And what if I can't stand Mireille with her white skin among all our blackness? You want my opinion: well, I'm ashamed of my grandson with his skin that's neither black nor white. Go and tell her so. You can despise Ouleymatou and take a foreigner's part. But you're the only one to decide that way. Go and rot with your Mireille! Go and hug your child. You wouldn't be seen with your nephew, would you, a pitch-black girl like you!'

Soukeyna spoke out, 'Why should I be ashamed of being seen out with Gorgui? In fact I take him for a walk every time I go to Mireille's.

Yaye Khady clasped her hands in horror. 'And you don't worry about everybody staring at you in a funny way?'

Soukeyna admitted, 'There are a few people with nothing better to do, who stare at us, like they might at a maid taking her employer's child out. But the whole street isn't up in arms, and they've got used to the situation now.' Soukeyna slammed the door and ran off to visit her friend.

Mireille put all her courage into surviving her ordeal. Her sister-in-law's affection and support helped her to hold out. She looked forward to her visits. With Soukeyna to talk to, she found the grip on her throat relax a little.

However, Soukeyna never let slip any mention of the gossip about her brother's 'other life', no matter how much Mireille expounded on her misery. Soukeyna's heart was full of compassion but her lips remained sealed. Yet she knew the source of her friend's misery. This source had a face and a name.

But gradually, as Mireille's tears flowed endlessly, as black rings circled her eyes, as her cheeks lost their colour and her unkempt hair its sheen, in the face of all the ravages wrought by suffering, Soukeyna felt an irresistible urge to come to her friend's rescue.

Her heart was involved and she could no longer forgive Ousmane's double-dealing. She racked her brains for a way to save Mireille, a way to rescue her from the grip of this suffering which was tearing her to pieces and causing her to waste away.

Several times she had been on the verge of denouncing Ousmane's treachery and the affront to Mireille. Several times she had been restrained by the difficulty of crucifying another person. Then an idea occurred to her, went round and round in her head, circumventing all her scruples, sweeping away all her hesitations. Oh! What a good idea! By the ingenious means of letting Mireille know anonymously!

'Oh! Hurry! Hurry! Let's put an end to the usurper's marriage and let Mireille regain her beauty and her joy in living!'

Chance is apt to thwart the best-laid plans. Ousmane had built his double life on Mireille's isolation. He had told Boly, 'Mireille will never be any the wiser. The world she lives in is impervious to tittle-tattle . . .'

Ousmane's new family put up with his absences. Ouleymatou, happy beyond her wildest dreams, made no demands. She and her mother had forgotten the stench of drains overflowing with rotting refuse. No, this was not a dream. There they really were, settled in a brick house, without the whole family living promiscuously on top of each other, without the daily arguments. They no longer had to stint and save to add a little flavour to the insipid fare of the family meals. As her mother lay under her warm blankets, she no longer remembered the days when she had to get up in the chill of dawn, to go off to her food-stall at the market.

What cause could she have for complaint? Ouleymatou had two servants. One cleaned the house and did the washing, the other did the cooking. All she had to do was to be beautiful for her husband when he turned up. And Yaye Khady protected her home. She showed her gratitude by extravagant gifts, from a boubou for best wear to a woven pagne. Bowls of food found their way to Gibraltar, bowls of chicken, bowls of fruit, bowls of couscous, bowls of barbecued lamb. She seized every opportunity of pleasing Yaye Khady, and Yaye Khady proudly invited her women friends to witness how well her daughter-in-law treated her. She shared the contents of the enormous bowls of food among her admiring neighbours.

What could Ouleymatou Ngom complain about?

Ousmane came every day: in a free period between classes, at lunchtime, every night. The bedroom door was bolted. Incense worked its intoxication. A new pregnancy became apparent.

As for Mireille, entangled in a spider's web of anguish, she hugged her son more closely to her, feeling him her only link with the world.

But fate foils the best-laid plans. Here it took the form of an anonymous letter which Mireille found in her pigeon-hole at school.

It warned her, '*You have got a Senegalese co-wife. If you want to know more about her, follow your husband.*'

Mireille read the words over and over again. In spite of her feeling of disgust, she examined the scrap of paper. The shape of the letters and their contorted down-strokes reminded her of familiar hand-writing. She racked her brain . . . And suddenly her suspicion became a certainty: it was Soukeyna's writing! This was the way her little friend had found of coming to her rescue, while freeing her conscience. The fact that the letter had been placed in her pigeon-hole at the school which Soukeyna attended, gave the game away.

She was caught in a double stranglehold: equally shocked by the letter's revelation and the course of action it advised, which her upbringing made her despise.

She collapsed under the strain and had to stay in bed. Her illness did not stop Ousmane in his comings and goings. Soukeyna, anxious and devoted, rushed to her bedside.

For a whole week Mireille thrashed about from one decision to another, alternatively accepting and rejecting the advice given in the letter. When she was well enough to get up she realised that the letter had got the better of her scruples. It introduced a new phase in her existence.

Mireille pulled herself together, her determined nature having triumphed over her immediate distress. Her relationship with Soukeyna was no longer so easy, as the girl seemed to be silently imploring her to reveal her intentions. But Mireille said nothing.

All alone, she built up her war strategy, reading the letter over and over to drain the very dregs of its bitter message. She needed to justify her course of action to her conscience which could not condone spying.

She must proceed systematically. A double life necessitates expenses. She must first scrutinise the bank account! They had opened this account with her own savings which she had transferred from France, and the couple's joint earnings were paid direct into it. One glance sufficed to measure the extent of the financial disaster. The figures left her speechless. Large unexplained sums had been withdrawn with increasing frequency. For what purpose? Ousmane continued to receive from her the money he needed for personal expenses. He did not smoke. He did not drink. She herself remitted every month to Djibril Gueye the sum they had agreed on for the family's maintenance. So? The massive withdrawals transformed her doubts into certainty.

She made her way to a taxi rank. She heard her own voice negotiating with the driver of the first car. She gave him her own address and got in. When they arrived, Mireille alighted but the taxi did not drive off. She had instructed the driver to wait for Ousmane Gueye to come home and then to follow him when he left again.

10

Ousmane Gueye came back from work. As usual, at this time, he had a quick wash and came out of the bathroom drying his face with his pyjama trousers which he threw down on an armchair. As usual he repeated, 'You can have your lunch. I'll eat later. I've got to go out for a few minutes. I'll be back.'

He was off and out of the door in a flash.

'A few minutes'? Mireille was sure she wouldn't see him again till the evening, for an hour or two, before he was off again with some more or less plausible excuse.

Mireille did not even look up from her newspaper. Her heart missed a beat. Her conscience revolted at the 'solution' she had found. But flouted as she was, she felt she existed in a zone where anything was permitted. She imagined the taxi following Ousmane's Peugeot. She would soon know. Five minutes! A quarter of an hour! Twenty minutes! Half an hour! An hour! Finally the bell rang. She opened the door. The face of the taxi driver she had engaged that morning was framed in the opening.

'I know where the gentleman went.'

'Good,' said Mireille. 'Come back this evening as arranged. We'll follow him together.'

She paid handsomely for this first service.

That evening the taxi followed the black Peugeot as it drove off fast, its indicators flashing in the darkness, bearing Ousmane off to his love-life.

The taxi parked a little way from the 504. Ousmane was smiling as he alighted.

How many months was it since she had seen him smile?

He entered a house surrounded by flowers. Hours passed, which seemed an eternity to Mireille consumed with jealousy.

Ousmane emerged, carrying a little boy with a shaved head, the spitting image of Gorgui. Ouleymatou followed, highly made up, her swollen belly protruding. She got in beside Ousmane who had put the child in the back and carefully locked the doors.

The car revved up. The couple alighted at Gibraltar, under Mireille's horrified eyes. But she was not just anyone. Coming from a family where breeding involved self-control, she could not make a spectacle of herself.

The couple reappeared, in good company. Yaye Khady was carrying the black child on her hip. With her free hand she tickled the baby who laughed just like Gorgui laughed when he was carried and cuddled like that.

'So, there's no end to the treachery!' In Mireille's eyes, all these people, entangled in their web of deceit, were completely disgusting.

Time and again she made use of the services of the taxi-driver, whom she generously remunerated . . . And one edifying scene followed another. The girl apppeared in a succession of outfits; the mannikin with the shaven head always accompanied them.

One evening, Ousmane's hand had openly fondled the tart's backside, in the street. Instead of repulsing him, the black woman had giggled and stuck out her behind.

The area round the house stank of incense and echoed with the joyful sounds of praise-singers. Little white pagnes, loin-clothes that African women wear as petticoats, fluttered on the washing-lines, evidence of the care the 'tart' lavished on her sex-life. They seemed to mock Mireille.

Ouleymatou's mother sat around with the neighbours, idly gossiping.

The more Mireille observed, the more she realised how estranged her husband had grown. A powerful magnetism was at work, dragging him back to his own world. And she wondered at her own efforts to adapt and forget her own background. The songs she used to sing? She no longer heard them except as a faint, distant echo. Her heart and her body had room only for Ousmane.

And Ousmane had not wanted to make any sacrifices. What was worse, every day he was widening the breach that separated them.

She remembered her father's anger: 'You are acquainted with "that object"?'

She admitted it. 'Ousmane was indeed "that object".'

Mireille discovered to her cost the ebb and flow of man's desire. Only the woman who momentarily occupies the heart and satisfies the sense of a man is important to him, monopolising his interest and his zest for conquest. Once he has satisfied his desire, he realises that 'the one and only' isn't up to the standard of her predecessors . . .

'But suppose Ousmane doesn't get tired of this one? What if this is the one, irrational, inexplicable infatuation which silences those who compare the new favourite with the woman who has been abandoned? I can't find any reasonable explanation; I can only think it must be the mysterious law of attraction. There's nothing extraordinary about this painted Negress!'

And Mireille agonised. 'The elements that make up love vary with every individual . . . Every love affair is different . . . Solutions that are right for some are no help in other cases . . . It's as impossible to pinpoint the moment when a feeling dies as it is to recognise the exact moment of its birth . . . What kills an emotion may have as little justification as what gives rise to it . . . It's difficult to stop a heart from sliding into the abyss of indifference . . .'

Mireille discovered to her cost how quickly man's desire burns itself out. She went to endless lengths to refurbish her armoury of seduction and win back Ousmane. She brushed her hair till it shone, rouged her cheeks, outlined her eyebrows and eyelashes. She drowned herself in costly perfumes: the little packets of incense which Ouleymatou bought at the market for the ridiculous price of twenty-five francs, cancelled out all her efforts.

It was agreed by many people that the *Toubab* wife had her good points: 'She's good-looking, intelligent, with a sweet nature, and she's in love with her husband.' But these virtues carried little weight with Ousmane's conscience.

And Mireille suffered. She tried to keep her suffering in harness throughout her lonely days and nights. She dragged herself from her bed to the bathroom, from the bathroom to her classes, from her classes back to the kitchen. Only the child could draw a smile from her, her sole source of comfort and affection. Her nerves were a-quiver; she was troubled with numbness in her feet; she clung on with iron determination not to break down.

She was haunted by the picture of the couple she had followed in the taxi. Gradually her store of courage and resistance was eroded entirely. In her imagination she pictured the amorous frolics from which she was excluded. She was mortified by the glimpses she had of erotic pleasures, which took place to her detriment. Made worse by the fact that nobody made any bones about commenting in her presence on the hot blood of black women. The woman she had spied upon reeked of experience in the arts of love.

Every night, every second, at school, at the market, her ears rang ceaselessly, everywhere, to the painted Negress's sniggers. She could not open her eyes without seeing Ousmane fondling those deliberately provocative plump buttocks.

Mireille kept tight control on her misery. She knew its extent. She measures its violence. Before she had known for sure, before she had had the evidence of her own eyes, Ousmane's infidelity had seemed a passing fancy. But now . . .

She wished she could run away from the aridity of her married life and go back to her parents. The prodigal daughter should be able to find forgiveness.

But . . . she had a son whom she loved. She searched his face for his father's finely chiselled features, which she had recognised in the other woman's child, to torture her with the memory. And so her thoughts swung from optimism to bitterness and back.

'Would my father accept a little coloured child in his very correct world? Could my father forget the affront to his dignity?'

'He seems to have bowed to the inevitable,' Yvette had written to her.

They might have welcomed Mireille back, without the child. But the coloured child existed, an embarrassing piece of evidence. He was there insatiably curious, searching for knobs to unscrew, lids to take off. He was there with his terracotta skin, all innocence and astonishment. Stamping his feet, he refused to wear the yellow jersey that matched his shorts. He looked at Mireille with his mischievous little eyes.

'Poor little thing!' and Mireille picked him up and put him on her lap to dress him. His tiny hands grabbed at her long hair that fell around him. 'Oh yes, I must stay, for his sake.'

The choice was a difficult one. One which Mireille found degrading.

'Not to deprive the child of his father is an unsound argument, as the child doesn't exist when one gets married. The child is supposed to strengthen the ties of a couple. He's supposed to bind them more closely. By himself, he cannot fill a wife's heart. He is not enough to satisfy a man. He can be a link? Yes.' She acknowledged, 'Children's lives are more miserable with an estranged couple than if they live with one parent alone, in an atmosphere of peace!'

Mireille was worried.

'The child argument doesn't hold water. Many humiliated wives use this excuse to camouflage their own lack of will-power. And with faces bathed in tears, these mothers protest how ill-used they are. But the reason they do not leave is cowardice, fear of assuming responsibility for themselves. They are kept prisoner by the habit of not thinking for themselves, not taking any decisions, not seeing with their own eyes, of letting others take over. It's not long before they crumble. They are eaten up with suffering. They don't know the meaning of liberty.'

She decided that she must survive.

So her great pride was not buried beneath the ruins of her marriage; it was galvanised into new life, giving new force to her resistance. She had been bent, but not crushed. She held her head high again, refusing to be the target for her countryfolk's derision. For the world of tea-parties could be vicious, as the guests, greedy for scandal, accompanied the tinkling of teaspoons with ironic comments!

She could imagine it: 'Have you heard the latest? Mireille's back from her escapade! Her nigger's thrown her out!' 'The rebellious bird has lost a few feathers and been packed off home with a black chick under her wing!' But above all, she could hear her father's ranting and raving, as he tugged harder than ever at his braces. Made a new man by the chance to say 'I told you so!' Delighting in his victory, mercilessly deriding his wife's mute distress!

'Ah, ha! Your daughter! Repudiated! Like a common object!

'Ah, ha! You see what happens when you disregard traditions of dignity!

'Ah, ha! It seems her son's got a hell of a sunburn! So the Negro ran off with a Negress! Ah, ha!'

In a country where self-interest is a way of life, where cowardly backbiting is the order of the day, the failure of her escapade would make her a laughing-stock. She could hope for no tolerance, no compassion to soothe her wounds. So she opted to suffer the fire of her anguish, rather than be exposed to an icy indifference or an aching paralysis of the soul. Here, to be sure, her values would be threatened every day; she would be humiliated, degraded by rejection! Here, too, there would be the affront to her dignity of a pretence at patience and feigned serenity! But, bewitched and ungrateful as Ousmane was, she would be living, feeling beside him, that sovereign power he still possessed to awaken her whole being.

She would live, she would fight, upheld by an ideal that did not sink to its knees. Her love and her pride together collected the crumbs of her dead happiness, to build with them some elements of hope. While her reason still argued the pros and cons, while her conscience told her that she must leave, her love and her pride refused to yield an inch of the territory they had won. Pathetically Mireille chose to stay. She attributed no greatness to her attitude. Her choice was not an evasion nor cowardice, but the only possible choice for a woman in love . . . for a woman with a black child on her hands . . . for a woman who has burnt her bridges behind her.

'And, when all's said and done, black men are not the only ones who are unfaithful to their wives!'

11

Mireille no longer laughed, Mireille no longer spoke, Mireille no longer ate, Mireille no longer slept. The orange sitting-room remained unswept, where she sat waiting every day for her faithless husband to return. Suffering had become an integral part of the rhythm of her existence.

And one evening, in an attempt to evoke her dead happiness, she took out of their hiding-place the letters her husband had written to her during their long engagement.

But the expressions of love were powerless to heal her pain. At what moment then, finding no more place to wound her body, did her persistent agony spill over to flood her brain and drown her reason? At what moment did her agonising suffering precipitate her into madness? The meretricious words of love jolted her mental distress. The lying words mocked her. Promises deliberately violated turned into hideous serpents that twined around her.

Oh! These letters from a false deceiver! From a dirty nigger! How could she have been taken in by them? Instead of the promised happiness, only the bitter taste of tears. Deprived of the joys of the flesh, for the benefits of the black woman, whose swollen belly proclaimed the satisfaction of her needs, Mireille stood naked in front of her mirror, searching for physical imperfections that could put off Ousmane. She saw a stranger reflected there . . .

She returned to the letters. Quick, where is the glue! She must exhibit the remains of her dream and her illusions like trophies to tell the whole world she had been loved. Quick, the glue! The glue, quick!

In one corner the letter in which Ousmane swore, '*I shall never love anyone but you, as long as I live.*'

Quick, the glue! The glue, quick!

Under this original painting, another epistle in which he cried, '*You, my "Blanche", you my "Blonde", how I miss you!*'

Quick, the glue! The glue, quick!

She giggled hysterically as she looked for a suitable place to stick the note in which Ousmane declared, '*Without you, life has no relish.*'

Quick, the glue! The glue, quick!

She climbed onto a stool and stuck this paper to the lamp shade.

Quick, the glue! The glue, quick!

She darted here and there, still naked. Her loose hair danced about her shoulders. Her son was crying in the next room. She abandoned her pot of glue and went instinctively to pick him up, singing a lullaby that Yaye Khady sang to him, dangling him on her knees, on the rare occasions when she held him:

'*Gnouloule Khessoule! Gnouloule Khessoule!*'

One of her pupils had told her the words meant, 'Not black! Not white!'

A violent surge of resentment flooded over her and she decreed, 'There's no place in this world for the *Gnouloule Khessoule!* A world of filthy bastards! A world of liars! You, my child, you're going to leave this world! *Gnouloule Khessoule!*'

She dissolved a handful of sleeping tablets in a cup of water and when the child opened his mouth to cry she poured the poisonous liquid down his throat. She was still giggling, imitating Yaye Khady's mocking voice, '*Gnouloule Khessoule! Gnouloule Khessoule!*'

She strutted around the sitting-room. The letters hung there, their fluttering taunting her with her betrayed hopes. At the sight of them new waves of fury surged through her, destroying the last traces of lucidity that hung by a slender thread from her consciousness.

Mireille went to the kitchen and came back with a carving knife which she sharpened as she yelled, '*Gnouloule Khessoule! Gnouloule Khessoule!*'

She fell exhausted onto the couch, dropping the knife which slipped between the cushions. There had been no sound in the flat as her sanity deserted her. The child slept the drugged sleep from which he would never awaken.

The hours passed. In his other home, Ousmane Gueye was enjoying the last transports of a night of love, and could scarcely drag himself from his black wife's side, as he pressed his ear to her belly, listening with delight to the beating heart of his unborn child.

The sky grew light with the coming of the dawn. Finally she heard the screeching tyres as the car braked. A door slammed! Steps in the hallway! A key turning in the lock! A drowsy Ousmane Gueye was greeted by a dishevelled naked woman screaming, 'Dirty nigger! Liar! Cheat! Adulterer! It's better with your nigger woman, isn't it? Answer me! You love your little Blackie better than your *Gnouloule Khessoule!*'

Ousmane stared open-eyed. What enemy had leaked a word of

advice to his wife? Who had denounced him and seen that his betrayal reached his wife's ears? His friends had warned him. He had taken no notice of their admonitions. Blinded by love and sexual desire, he had believed in his own strength. And now the evidence of his heinous crime confronted him in Mireille's contorted face.

'The *Gnouloule Khessoule* is dead!'

And Mireille pushed him towards the cradle: Gorgui was ice-cold to his father's touch.

Ousmane Gueye looked up sadly, in a daze. The brutal truth was obvious to him: Mireille had gone mad. The cold, still body of his son was eloquent. The work of a madwoman! He looked around him. His letters hung fluttering. Mireille was still screaming, 'Filthy nigger! Dirty traitor! Adulterer! Cheat!'

She was trembling. She hiccupped. Fear triggered off a belated surge of reason in Ousmane's mind. A light of humanity finally pierced the thick darkness. A feeling of nausea and self-disgust flooded over him. It was he who had been mad and had contaminated Mireille. Only madness could explain his blindness and his actions. If carried to extremes, so that it tramples pity and compassion underfoot, then commitment goes beyond the bounds of reason.

Of what uncompromising dogma had he set himself up as the apostle, in the land where the water-pitcher passes from hand to hand and from mouth to mouth without repugnance? What had his father taught? A generous heart, pity and charity: '*Nit, nit, modi garabam!*' Man, man is his own remedy! Had he thought what he was doing? Unthinkingly to take a beautiful young woman, intelligent, virtuous, hungry for affection and offering love in abundance, and turn her into a fury. And what fury! Her fury that was still shrieking insults at him . . .

A man's whole life can flash through his mind in a few seconds! His honeymoon spent in the mountain hotel, where huge logs burnt in an ancient fireplace. His first nights with Mireille, a feast of roses: the rosy curves of her breasts, on which disordered lace cast bluish shadows, the pinkish mauve of her nightdress and all the rubescent shades left by the mark of his fingers on her milky skin. How his heart beat fit to burst! His senses replete with profound, intense happiness! The irritations of daily existence had drowned these colours and sensations in oblivion . . . Ouleymatou emerged, a symphony of soothing shadows accompanying his feverish quests, an intoxicating smell of millet-flour, escaping from the mortars of his childhood, a water-vessel held in perfect balance by her potter's hands? His whole life flashed by in a few seconds! Djibril Gueye's magnanimity . . . Yaye Khady's malice . . . Boly . . . Ali . . . Coumba . . . Marième . . . Gorgui! Gorgui dead! Ouleymatou's son with his laughing eyes! Of what sex, his unborn child?

Visible to her alone, as it lay between the cushions, the blade of the knife beckoned Mireille with its will o' the wisp gleam. She seized it and the seconds lengthened in the face of madness and the premonition of death.

In his mental confusion Ousmane had no time to call on the instinct for self-preservation. Mireille had already attacked him. He was handicapped by two deep wounds in his shoulder and right arm, as he struggled desperately to disarm his wife. There seemed no escape. She stabbed and stabbed again. Madness lent her strength to wield the knife. Ousmane staggered towards the front door which he had not had time to shut behind him. On the landing he shouted with his last remaining strength, 'Genevieve! Guillaume!' before he collapsed.

Guillaume sat up with a start. Still entangled in the bedclothes, he shook Genevieve hard. 'Did you hear? At Beauty and the Beast's. I told you so. Beauty was unhappy. I only hope . . .'

Mireille wandered to and fro on the landing, wild-eyed, the carving-knife still in her hand. Ousmane Gueye lay on the floor. Mireille did not seem to see him as she continued walking aimlessly to and fro. A scarlet song welled up from Ousmane's wounds, the scarlet song of lost hopes.

The two neighbours called the police and an ambulance and sat waiting for help. They lived through the most terrible minutes of their stay in Africa.

Early the next morning after this tragic occurrence a police car was sent to Gibraltar to wrest Djibril Gueye from his dawn prayers.

Yaye Khady accompanied him, filled with apprehension. The virtuous Djibril could find nothing in his conscience to explain this summons.

'What evidence do they want from me? What crime has been committed?' He feigned optimism to calm Yaye Khady while his heart beat faster with worry, as he thought of Ousmane driving 'that lethal machine, dispenser of brutal death'.

Djibril Gueye was shown into the office of a courteous young man who left his imposing desk and came to sit beside him.

'You are Djibril Gueye, ex-service man, father of Ousmane Gueye, the high-school teacher?'

'Yes,' he gasped.

Then the young inspector told him the horrifying story. With every word he spoke, Djibril seemed to shrink. He hammered on the floor with his stick.

At the end of the nightmare account, Djibril murmured a prayer.

'Acho dou en la illa ha illala

Acho dou en Mohamed Rossoloula.

I declare that God is God.

I declare that Mohamed is his Prophet.

God has decided thus, he who is Master of all men and all things, Master of the ordering of facts and time.'

The inspector added, 'Ousmane is in hospital. He is said to be out of danger.'

Djibril Gueye found the strength to inquire, 'And Mireille?'

'The ambulance men did not have any difficulty in subduing her. An anonymous letter found in her handbag explains the drama. A French couple, their neighbours, have given evidence.'

The shock was hard. And Djibril gasped again, 'What will become of Mireille?'

'The French Embassy have been informed and they are taking the matter in hand,' the inspector concluded.

There remained an even harder battle to be waged: Yaye Khady was waiting outside. So he rose to his feet and composed his features.

Yaye Khady was trembling. Her eyes were dilated. Whatever could this atrocious news be?

Djibril walked heavily, enclosed in the rigid armature of his burdensome secret, clinging more tightly than ever to his stick for support.

He lowered himself slowly onto the bench on the veranda reserved for visitors. Today he forgot his usual care to make his game leg comfortable when he sat down.

'Allah Akbar! Allah Akbar!

God is great! God is great!

He struggled out of the darkness which enfolded him.

'Lane-la? Lane-la? What is it? What is it?' implored Yaye Khady.

'Lane-la? Lane-la?' Djibril Gueye echoed.

It was difficult to establish a tragic dialogue between a father who feared the amputation of the pride of his existence and a mother whose maternal instinct made her as unapproachable as a lioness in labour.

'*Lane-la- Lane-la?*'

Yaye Khady crouched, broken, in Djibril's arms. The breast of the disciple of God shook with heavy sobs, which, though he stifled them, continued to break out afresh.

'*Lane-la? Lane-la*'

Slowly Djibril let fall the words of a wise, traditional saying:

' *Kou wathie sa toundeu, tound'eu boo fèke mou tasse.*

When one abandons one's own hill, the next hill which one climbs will crumble.'

He closed his eyes and murmured, 'The *Toubab* has gone mad and tried to kill Ousmane.'

'*Lane-la? Lane-la?*' Yaye Khady intoned.

'*Lane-la? Lane-la?*'

The melancholy duet swelled to a chorus. The tragic chorus was swelled by new supporters.

'*Lane-la? Lane-la?*'

A crowd gathered around them.

'*Lane-la? Lane-la?*'

They cried in sympathy:

'*Lane-la? Lane-la?*'

Glossary and notes

Topography

Except for a short episode set in Paris, the action of Mariama Bâ's novel takes place in Dakar, the capital of her native Senegal, in the Cape Verde Peninsular.

Grand-Dakar is a sprawling, poor, working-class area on the outskirts of the city.

Usine Niari Talli is a district in Grand-Dakar which derives its name from the two parallel arteries which run through it and the proximity of a biscuit factory (Usine de Biscuiterie)

Gibraltar is a district of subsidised dwellings, (similar to a council house estate), lying between the Port of Dakar and the Medina, which replaced a particularly bad slum area.

Guédiawaye is an outlying suburb of Dakar, on the coast. Apart from the explanation for its name that the author puts into the mouth of Boly (p48), some Senegalese believe the name to be a deformation of the English 'Get away!', as access to the area was so difficult.

Ouakam and *Pikine* are two townships situated on the outskirts of Dakar.

Society, traditional and religious customs

caste system: All main Senegalese ethnic groups are divided into castes. Traditionally, marriage across the caste barrier was impossible, and is still frowned upon. The highest caste comprises the descendants of princes and *Guer* (nobles); the lowest, artisans, such as jewellers, weavers, dyers, etc. Poverty or riches bear no relationship to caste.

compound (*concession*): a group of huts constituting one family's habitation.

dédelé: spell by which a woman attracts a man and makes him fall in love with her.

diali: a poet and musician, a *griot*.

francs: the sums referred to are CFA (Communauté Financière d'Afrique) the currency of most of Francophone West Africa, 50 francs CFA = 1 French franc.

gor-djiguène: literally, 'man-woman'; a homosexual and transvestite, often employed as 'housekeeper', sometimes as procurer, or in other menial functions.

griot (fem. *griote*): professional musicians, chroniclers, praise-singers. The *griot* belongs to one of the lowest castes, just higher than the slave.

Guer: a man of noble origins and caste.

'hut-brothers': men who have undergone circumcision rites together and whose friendship has thus been sealed for life.

jinnee: a spirit, able to appear in human and animal forms and having supernatural power over humans (see *rab*).

Lebu: an ethnic group inhabiting the Cape Verde peninsula, virtually indistinguishable from the Wolof who comprise 35% of the population of Senegal.

Linguère: a woman of noble birth (cf. *Guer*).

Mandjaque: an ethnic group from the Casamance region of Senegal, whose weaving is much prized.

marabout: a Muslim teacher and holy man. He also prepares talismans for protection against dangers of all kinds. It is sometimes suspected that his assistance is sought to gain certain ends by supernatural means.

Mourides: an Islamic brotherhood whose members hope to attain saintliness through total obedience to the guidance of their marabouts.

ndeup: traditionally a pagan exorcism dance frowned upon by Islamic leaders, performed especially among the Lebu, by a healer and a number of initiates. Now used as a healing trance incorporated into modern psychiatric practice.

pinth: the traditional village general assembly or 'palaver'. Now also used as group therapy in psychiatric treatment.

rab: a type of jinnee; invisible, supernatural creatures of either sex who can protect or harm mortals, particularly by 'possession' of those who neglect or displease them.

soutura: quality of decency, respectability, sobriety.

talibé: a marabout's young pupil and disciple. He lives with his master who sends him out begging for food and clothing.

Toubab: name by which whites are designated in Francophone West Africa.

tour: a type of jinnee.

'turn': in a polygamous Islamic marriage, the period when a wife can expect her husband to sleep with her and during which she is responsible for cooking for the household and doing his washing.

Yaye: mother.

Clothing

boubou: a sort of voluminous caftan worn as an outer garment by men and women, impeccably starched if made of cotton; women often wear gauzy, man-made fabrics which float elegantly around the body.

djité laye: a very short loin-cloth or *pagne* which women wear as an underpetticoat; often combined with strings of beads around the hips for sexual titillation.

gongo: a strong musky perfume, to which aphrodisiac powers are attributed.

pagne: a length of woven material worn draped around the waist.

Food and drink

couscous: basic dish made from granulated millet steamed over broth.

foufou: a dish made of *gombo* (an edible plant) and palm-oil, to accompany couscous or fish with rice.

kinkeliba: an aromatic and refreshing infusion.

m'boum: sauce made with cabbage-leaves and ground peanuts, to accompany couscous.

Moorish tea: a strong mint tea, brewed in a metal teapot and drunk after meals as an aid to digestion.

oba, thiof, yaboye: types of deep-sea fish.

sanglé: a beverage made from millet-flour, water and sugar.

Musical terms

back: a litanic chant, a praise-song.

balafon: a kind of xylophone.

khalam: a four-stringed guitar.

kora: a type of harp with between 16 to 32 strings.

gorong, ndeud, sabar, tama: different types of drum.

I wish to acknowledge the friendly assistance of Ahmed Sheikh with the explanation of certain Wolof words.

Dorothy S. Blair

Other Titles available

Longman African Writers

Tides	I Okpewho	0 582 10276 6
Of Men and Ghosts	K Aidoo	0 582 22871 9
Flowers and Shadows	B Okri	0 582 03536 8
The Victims	I Okpewho	0 582 26502 9
Call Me Not a Man	M Matshoba	0 582 00242 7
Dilemma Of a Ghost/Anowa	A A Aidoo	0 582 27602 0
Our Sister Killjoy	A A Aidoo	0 582 30845 3
No Sweetness Here	A A Aidoo	0 582 26456 1
Between Two Worlds	A Tlali	0 582 28764 2
The Children of Soweto	M Mzamane	0 582 26434 0
A Son Of The Soil	W Katiyo	0 582 02656 3
The Stillborn	Z Alkali	0 582 26432 4
The Life of Olaudah Equiano	P Edwards	0 582 26473 1
Sundiata	D T Niane	0 582 26475 8
The Last Duty	I Okpewho	0 582 78535 9
Hungry Flames	M Mzamane	0 582 78590 1
Scarlet Song	M Ba	0 582 26455 3
Fools	N Ndebele	0 582 78621 5
The Park	J Matthews	0 582 26435 9
Sugarcane With Salt	J Ng'ombe	0 582 05204 1
Study Guide to 'Scarlet Song'	M Ba	0 582 21979 5
African New Voices	S Brown *et al*	0 582 24996 1

All these titles are available or can be ordered from your local book-seller. For further information on these titles, and on study guides available, contact your local Longman agent or Longman International Education, Addison Wesley Longman Limited, Edinburgh Gate, Harlow, Essex, CM20 2JE, England.